Using Data-Based Processes to Create Sustainable Change in Your School and Community

Rooted in the idea that education is an open, dynamic system composed of a continuous interchange of components, this eye-opening resource presents a data-based, process-focused framework for solving the unique problems of your specific school or system. Contrary to popular "quick fix" and intervention-based strategies, this book reflects the holistic process required for educational reform that can be sustained and continuously improved over time. With a focus on determining and implementing solutions, the book features vignettes and brief case studies, reflective questions, activity matrices, and helpful infographics that bring key ideas to life. *Using Data-Based Processes to Create Sustainable Change* is key reading for school and district leaders, administrators, and professional development organizations interested in supporting the development of a critical mass of collaborative faculty and staff.

Christan R. Pankiewicz, Ph.D., is an Associate Professor of Special Education and Early Childhood Special Education, a Board Certified Behavior Analyst, and an Educational Consultant with Propel Inclusive Education.

Heather L. Walter, Ed.D., is an Assistant Professor of Special Education, a Senior Scholar at the Center for the Advancement of Wellbeing, and an Educational Consultant with Propel Inclusive Education.

Katherine Mitchem, Ph.D., is a national professional development specialist and a Board Certified Behavior Analyst. Dr. Mitchem has certification and teaching experience in secondary education, multicategorical special education, and autism.

Other Eye On Education Books Available from Routledge
(www.routledge.com/eyeoneducation)

Improving Your School One Week at a Time
Building the Foundation for Professional Teaching and Learning, Second Edition
Jeffrey Zoul and Spiri Diamantis Howard

Finding Your Leadership Edge
Balancing Assertiveness and Compassion in Schools
Brad Johnson and Jeremy Johnson

Redesigning Special Education Systems through Collaborative Problem Solving
A Guidebook for School Leaders
Michelle Brenner and Kelly Miller

Cultivating Behavioral Change in K–12 Students
Team-Based Intervention and Support Strategies
Marty Huitt and Gail Tolbert

Invest in Your Best
9 Strategies to Grow, Support, and Celebrate Your Most Valuable Teachers
Todd Whitaker, Connie Hamilton, Joseph Jones, and T.J. Vari

Using Data-Based Processes to Create Sustainable Change in Your School and Community

A Step-by-Step Guide for Leaders in Education

Christan R. Pankiewicz, Heather L. Walter, and Katherine Mitchem

NEW YORK AND LONDON

Designed cover image: shutterstock

First published 2025
by Routledge
605 Third Avenue, New York, NY 10158

and by Routledge
4 Park Square, Milton Park, Abingdon, Oxon, OX14 4RN

Routledge is an imprint of the Taylor & Francis Group, an informa business

© 2025 Taylor & Francis

The right of Christan R. Pankiewicz, Heather L. Walter, and Katherine Mitchem to be identified as authors of this work has been asserted in accordance with sections 77 and 78 of the Copyright, Designs and Patents Act 1988.

All rights reserved. No part of this book may be reprinted or reproduced or utilised in any form or by any electronic, mechanical, or other means, now known or hereafter invented, including photocopying and recording, or in any information storage or retrieval system, without permission in writing from the publishers.

Trademark notice: Product or corporate names may be trademarks or registered trademarks, and are used only for identification and explanation without intent to infringe.

ISBN: 978-1-032-67344-8 (hbk)
ISBN: 978-1-032-62738-0 (pbk)
ISBN: 978-1-032-67345-5 (ebk)

DOI: 10.4324/9781032673455

Typeset in Palatino
by KnowledgeWorks Global Ltd.

To Anna, you have inspired me to bring this team of experts and amazing collaborators together and continue to provide my why for this work. To my family Oliver, Anna, Ethan, Zoey, and Owen, thank you for your support and allowing me to "step away" when needed to bring this project to completion. To Oliver, thank you for not only being my life partner but also my thought partner, my sounding board, and providing such thoughtful feedback. To my mom, thank you for being my advocate throughout my school experience and inspiring me to be an educator. I know that the challenges I overcame and the successes I have experienced would not be possible without you. To my dad, Bob, thank you for your love and always being available to listen and provide support. To all the educators, systems, research participants, families, children, and students I have had the honor to partner with, thank you for all that you have and continue to teach me. To my dear golden retriever, Lily, thank you for staying by my side as we wrote, edited, and wrote some more together.

—Christan R. Pankiewicz

Elon, Thank you for always being the most remarkable husband, father and teacher. To my three boys, Jake, Ethan, and Sam- You inspire me to be the best mother and educator I can be. You truly are the experts in the field, and I am so proud of who you are and who you will become.

To my grandmother "Mema", who spent her entire career as the high school secretary, greeting generations of students as they walked into the building. The years I spent watching you build relationships was integral to my sense of being at a time when I was angry at the educational system and felt that I did not have a place within it. Your ability to connect with others in meaningful ways along with your sense of style has shaped who I am today. I am grateful for being able to spend so much time with you.

—Heather L. Walter

To my family, Tim, Daniel, Sophie, Samara, Reyna, and Alexi for that they continue to give me and teach me each day and for their love and support.

To all the brilliant educators and those in training who have inspired and taught me along the way.

—Katherine Mitchem

Contents

Meet the Authors viii
Preface x

1 The Need for This Book 1

2 Recognize the Need for Change and the Complexities
   of Change in Practice 9

3 The Systems Change Process 22

4 Collaboration and How It Connects with the System 27

5 Data-Based Needs 42

6 Determine Solutions 57

7 Supporting Implementation of the Solution 70

8 Evaluate the Process and Solution 92

9 Sustain Change and Celebrate Success 103

   Appendix 111

Meet the Authors

Christan R. Pankiewicz, Ph.D., is an Associate Professor of Special Education and Early Childhood Special Education, a Board Certified Behavior Analyst, and an Educational Consultant with Propel Inclusive Education. She has spent over the last 20 years working in communities, schools, and higher education with a focus on supporting educators and families to achieve goals. Her research is focused on identifying effective professional development processes and systems, ultimately to improve child and student outcomes. She has maintained strong partnerships with schools and community systems to support them in achieving their systemic goals. To date, she has published over 60 peer-reviewed publications, book chapters, and informational briefs, is engaged in state and federally funded projects, and teaches courses in special education, behavior analysis, research methods, and early childhood special education.

Heather L. Walter, Ed.D., is an Assistant Professor of Special Education, a Senior Scholar for the Center for Advancement of Wellbeing, and an Educational Consultant. Her expertise builds upon over 15 years in diverse education settings cultivating the unique strengths of individuals, and communities by partnering and providing support in the recruitment and retention of highly qualified educators and the wellbeing and sustainability of educational systems. Her primary goal is to support those who care for and educate children and youth in making evidence-based decisions that close the opportunity gap – that leads to thriving and balanced educational outcomes. Walter is engaged in federally funded research, has published in both practitioner and research journals, as well as sits on local, regional, and national education organizations. Dr. Walter has been recognized for the 2021 Dissertation Award in Mixed Methods for the American Educational Research Association (AERA) and her contributions to policy research through the Society for Research in Child Development (SRCD).

Katherine Mitchem, Ph.D., is a national professional development specialist and a Board Certified Behavior Analyst. Dr. Mitchem has certification and teaching experience in secondary education, multicategorical special education, and autism. She was an Endowed Chair in Special Education at the California University of Pennsylvania where she directed an OSEP Preservice Training Improvement grant and co-directed a series of technology grants and an Institute for Education Sciences Project, Electronic Performance Support Systems (EPSS) as Assistive Technologies: Improving Secondary and Transition Outcomes for Secondary Students with Mild Disabilities. Her research and practice have focused on collaborating with school districts to ensure positive outcomes for students through effective and inservice teacher development and support and strategic use of technology to support educators and learners.

Preface

The word "change" pushes us to think beyond what we may perceive ourselves to be comfortable and capable. Metaphors are meant to shape our understanding of complex issues. We need to reflect on our metaphors and our understanding of systems change. There is no perfect metaphor to capture its essence and meaning when it pertains to education and systems change. Choose your metaphor carefully as our metaphors project our different perceptions of education. For example,

- Education is a journey, a ladder
- Schools are gardens, prisons, or assembly line factories
- Teachers are doctors who individually diagnose students
- School is a job, school is play, school is for academics, and school should be holistic
- Students are like empty buckets and teachers pour knowledge into them

In this book, we provide a fresh perspective grounded in real education case studies and concrete analogies to illustrate a process to engage in systems change that is malleable to individual and contextual resources, needs, and goals. While the shiny new toy permeates throughout education in new technology, initiatives, strategies, and more, this book takes us back to the foundation: (1) people, (2) relationships, and context to intact innovative change. Change itself for the purpose of innovativeness or improving educational experiences is good. Everyone is going to have very different opinions, and their experiences from practice and theory may shape what they believe, how they interact, and how they implement ideas. Change must be intentional and purposeful as constant change can damage long-term performance, learning, and cause unnecessary stress and confusion.

This book provides a process for systems change to support innovation and impact in the educational context in which you reside ultimately enhancing student's social and academic outcomes. While it has never been easy to challenge what has always been done and what is comfortable, individually, a system of any kind, in any context is just the opposite – pulling individuals together who have different personalities, needs, goals, and dreams and placing them together in a high-intensity setting to problem-solve complex solutions in a changing and complex world for our most valuable asset – our children. While still challenging, working together in a team creates a sense of ownership, responsibility, and pride over accomplished goals, and when positive, can create lasting change.

While systems in themselves always try to preserve the status quo necessary, we believe the opposite is essential. As current consultants and coaches in the field, and previous educators within early intervention, preschool, elementary, secondary, and higher education settings, we recognize and have experienced the current challenges of working towards improving educational outcomes for all children and students across contexts.

We live in a time in which we count on educational professionals to be experts in their field but also not taken seriously enough to make individual or collective decisions that educators know are in the best interests of children, families, communities, and educational settings to produce young adults who can critically think, advocate for themselves and others, and foster positive self-identities and healthy reciprocal relationships with peers and adults alike. Unfortunately, we witnessed, far too many times, where the investment in a quick fix or belief that "one size fits all" never yielded the desired changes or results it intended. We have watched the pendulum swings of educational strategies and pedagogy. Our over two decades in education, with diverse (general and special education) and (urban, suburban, and rural) as well as our extensive research yielding well over 150 peer-reviewed research and practice-based articles, and over 300 presentations locally, regionally, nationally, and internationally, we feel that we are positioned to support you on this journey as we navigate your contexts, strengths, and needs together – with whatever perspectives, experiences, and identities you come to read this book with.

We are not writing to place value or lack of value on any of these in particular; instead, we are writing this book to provide a process and differentiated and contextualized strategies to facilitate systems change around a problem identified by a school system and its partners. This process-oriented approach allows individual school systems to reflect and choose the strategies that work for them and use their data to make informed decisions about their system that are more likely to yield desired changes or results. We hope that the benefits will be for all of us and the education system as a whole. We have more power than we realize to come and work together to enhance educational opportunities for all children.

1

The Need for This Book

According to the Institute of Educational Sciences School Pulse Data (2023), public schools are facing significant challenges that are inhibiting them from recruiting and retaining a qualified workforce and meeting the diverse needs of the students and families they serve (Chetty et al., 2014; Nguyen et al., 2020). Historically, the inability to retain a qualified workforce has been mostly due to retirement and/or an increase in student populations (Watlington et al., 2010). These reasons have shifted to educators prematurely leaving the field at unprecedented rates (Carver-Thomas & Darling-Hammond, 2017). This has left education systems significantly understaffed with approximately 8% of teachers leaving the profession, accounting for almost 90% of the annual teacher demand (Carver-Thomas & Darling-Hammond, 2017; Will et al., 2023). Turnover has a profound impact as it costs approximately $2.2 billion annually nationwide when educators leave the field rising to $4.9 billion per year when educators transfer schools or job placements (Watlington et al., 2010).

These numbers are highly relevant as teachers have consistently been identified as the most critical variable in shaping student outcomes, yet schools are experiencing significant challenges with recruiting and retaining career-ready educators. Research demonstrates the impact of turnover on both schools and students. Schools often respond to turnover by hiring inexperienced or unqualified teachers, increasing class sizes, or removing class options, all of which impact student outcomes (Sutcher et al., 2019). Students in schools with high turnover and inexperienced teachers are at an educational disadvantage (Kini & Podolsky, 2016), yet turnover impacts the achievement of all students. Turnover impacts a school's ability to engage in continuous collaboration and improvement (Guin et al., 2004; Ronfeldt et al., 2013). Indeed, these shortages manifest nationally in student outcomes (Castro et al., 2023). The average percentage of public-school students behind grade level beginning 2023–2024 was 44%. Sixty-eight percent of public schools reported being identified for a school improvement plan in at least one subject area, and 29% of public schools were identified for comprehensive support or additional targeted support.

Schools are not only faced with meeting the academic needs of students but also the increased need for mental health services. Sixty-nine percent of public schools reported that the percentage of students who have sought mental health services increased since the start of the COVID-19 pandemic. Twenty-nine percent of public schools reported that the percentage of staff who have sought mental health services increased since the start of the COVID-19 pandemic. When educators are unwell, their students' cortisol levels (stress) mirror those of their educators, which increase student stress, negatively impacting both teaching and learning (Jennings et al., 2017).

Furthermore, both qualitative and quantitative research has confirmed that educators (leaders and teachers) do not feel valued in their professions in the United States. Many leaders state that they feel caught in the middle of the system, with no support and with little resources to implement policies and practices, and teachers state that they work in negative school cultures with administrators who do not understand or respect their roles as experts in the field. For example, although the system values mental health in educational settings, the funds are student driven, not educator driven. Legislative initiatives such as the American Rescue Plan Act (2021) and the Bipartisan Safer Communities Act (2022) have allocated resources to school-based mental health programs for students (Prothero & Riser-Kositsky, 2022), but there are neither federal initiatives nor legislation for the increased well-being or development for educators to support students in the system, which we know is imperative for student outcomes. Additionally, the media has contributed to an overall distaste for the American educational system and a distrust in leaders and teachers with reports of "unqualified teachers" in schools, and teachers being held accountable and responsible for test scores and overall failing school ratings for teaching students that they have had in a classroom setting for less than a year. Therefore, when leaders and teachers feel disconnected, underprepared, undervalued, and ineffective in the domain of their practice, the quality of education is diminished and leaders and teachers are unable to partner together with families, and with students. Further, as burnout and dissatisfaction increase, and well-being decreases, this leaves educators to make difficult choices to exit the system (Mazzer & Rickwood, 2015).

Why Read This Book?

As education leaders, administrators, personnel, students, and families experience the implications of the challenges the education system faces, there is a critical need to engage in an effective process to address these challenges. This process should be focused on ensuring the diverse needs of children, students, families, educators, administrators, and leaders are met. This book provides a data-based and strategic process for problem-solving embedded within an open system change framework to facilitate sustainable change for improved academic and behavior outcomes for all children and students while ensuring educators, administrators, and leaders are valued for the unique perspectives and expertise they have within the systems change process. It provides practical information and tools to understand components of systems change, and to engage in a problem-solving process that includes defining the problem, identifying partners, conducting a needs assessment, generating and selecting solution(s), determining action steps, supporting implementation of solutions, evaluating progress, and sustaining change and celebrating success.

Why We Chose to Write This Book

As current consultants and coaches in the field, and previous educators within early intervention, preschool, elementary, secondary, and higher education settings, we recognize and have experienced the current challenges facing the community and schools, ranging from shortages of educators, difficulty replacing qualified staff to teach or maintain schools or substitutes to come in on an as-needed basis. Meanwhile, higher percentages of students are performing behind grade level post-pandemic and are seeking mental health services (Irwin et al., 2023). These issues contribute to a need for leaders to apply a process of systems change to make improvements within their schools, district, and/or community. We witnessed, far too many times, the investment in a quick fix or belief that "one size fits all" never yielded the desired changes or results. We recognize the post-pandemic struggles the field of education is experiencing with declining standardized test scores, an inability to maintain adequate numbers of qualified staff, and the general struggle with well-being.

Throughout our careers, we have watched the pendulum swings of educational strategies, programs, curricula, and practices. **We are not writing to place value or lack of value on any of these in particular; instead, we are writing this book to provide a process and differentiated and contextualized strategies to facilitate systems change around a problem identified by a school system and its partners. This process-oriented approach allows individual school systems to choose the strategies that work for them and use their data to make informed decisions about their system that are more likely to yield desired changes or results.** With this process, it is possible for multiple problems to be addressed simultaneously due to the systems thinking perspective presented that involves looking at the system, understanding the interconnected and interactive components of the system, both internally and externally, and using the information to guide the application of a process to effect systems change.

For Whom Are We Writing This Book?

We anticipate **education system leaders using this text district or region-wide** to plan and implement year-round systemic professional development to support the development and well-being of a critical mass of collaborative faculty and staff. **The outcomes will include a faculty and staff who are highly trained in identifying and defining problems in their context; sourcing and evaluating evidence-based strategies, solutions, and resources for best fit; having a voice in the solutions and strategies implemented; and then implementing and monitoring the progress of those strategies selected.** Ultimately, and most importantly, children and students will accelerate learning due to data-based implementation of the whole systems approach that considers the entire context including mental health and well-being.

This book encourages the use of data to help you see reality objectively and establish a shared vision; provides a systems change approach to help you engage in systems thinking and reflect and ask questions; addresses necessary interpersonal skills to effectively contribute to a collective team involved in systems change; and offers a systems problem-solving process with strategies and tools to guide you in applying data in defining the problem, conducting a needs assessment, generating and selecting solutions, determining action steps, and evaluating progress. The tools and resources we provide throughout the book are meant to provide a menu of options that allow teams to consider their specific context as we recognize that each system has different resources, challenges, and goals. Each chapter also includes reflection questions for teams to consider as they reflect upon the content within each chapter.

We also recognize that the information presented in this book is only the start, and when working with a diverse team of educators, administrators, students, and families, challenges will emerge. These challenges can create setbacks and even barriers to achieving the goals the team has identified within the systems change process. In each chapter, we include a table of potential change preventers

TABLE 1.1 Change Preventers and Facilitators

Change Preventers	Change Facilitators
Change preventers can include:	Change facilitators can include:
- Misunderstanding/misperception of job roles and resources between leaders and teachers - Unavailable or limited resources for training and teaching - Constant changes in curriculum - Perception that teachers are not experts in their field	- Clear communication of job roles and responsibilities of leaders and teachers and how each can work together - Understand policy decisions and implications on a state and national level and advocate with leaders and community members - Voice opinion in clear, and productive ways (i.e., reframe) about curricular choices - Educate families and communities by partnering and building strong relationships

and change facilitators to support teams in identifying potential resources to overcome these barriers (Table 1.1).

We also recognize the importance of language and how language can be used to create confusion or clarity. We use several terms throughout this book. To ensure clarity we have provided a list of definitions below.

Definitions

- ◆ Leader: Anyone who is committed to enhancing the current environment in which they interact. This can include a teacher, community worker, and/or administrator.
- ◆ Educator: Any individual responsible for the education of children and students (e.g., preschool teacher, elementary teacher, related service provider within an education setting).
- ◆ Systems: Interconnecting structures that are set up to promote the implementation of an action.
- ◆ Data-based process: Using information through measures such as surveys, conversations, and progress monitoring to inform decisions that are made.
- ◆ Sustainable change: Change that is feasible to maintain.

- Dynamic: Factors that stimulate change within a system.
- Partner/team/group/participants: Individuals who work together to support change.
- Wellness: A focused approach that targets one dimension of physical and mental health.
- Well-being: A multidimensional approach that focuses on multiple domains of health (physical, mental, spiritual, and financial) but balances both individual and environmental factors together to support holistic well-being.
- Children and students: We use the terms children and students as we recognize educators also work within communities where they may not be working with youth and young adults (ages 9 and up) students but rather children (birth to 8 years old).

Reflection Questions

1. What are features of your education setting that make your context unique?
2. What unique strengths and challenges do you perceive experiencing within your setting?

References

Carver-Thomas, D., & Darling-Hammond, L. (2017). *Teacher turnover: Why it matters and what we can do about it*. Learning Policy Institute.

Castro, A. J. (2023). Managing competing demands in a teacher shortage context: The impact of teacher shortages on principal leadership practices. *Educational Administration Quarterly*, *59*(1), 218–250. https://doi.org/10.1177/0013161X221140849

Chetty, R., Friedman, J. N., & Rockoff, J. E. (2014). Measuring the impacts of teachers II: Teacher value-added and student outcomes in adulthood. *American Economic Review*, *104*(9), 2633–2679. https://doi.org/10.1257/aer.104.9.2633

Guin, K. (2004). Chronic teacher turnover in urban elementary schools. *Education Policy Analysis Archives*, *12*(42), 1–30. https://doi.org/10.14507/epaa.v12n42.2004

Irwin, V., Wang, K., Tezil, T., Zhang, J., Filbey, A., Jung, J., ... Parker, S. (2023). Report on the Condition of Education 2023. NCES 2023-144. *National Center for Education Statistics*.

Jennings, P. A., Brown, J. L., Frank, J. L., Doyle, S., Oh, Y., Davis, R., Rasheed, D., DeWeese, A., DeMauro, A. A., Cham, H., & Greenberg, M. T. (2017). Impacts of the CARE for teachers program on teachers' social and emotional competence and classroom interactions. *Journal of Educational Psychology*, *109*(7), 1010–1028. https://doi.org/10.1037/edu0000187

Kini, T., & Podolsky, A. (2016). *Does teaching experience increase teacher effectiveness? A review of the research*. Learning Policy Institute.

Mazzer, K. R., & Rickwood, D. J. (2015). Teachers' role breadth and perceived efficacy in supporting student mental health. *Advances in School Mental Health Promotion*, *8*(1), 29–41. https://doi.org/10.1080/1754730X.2014.978119

Nguyen, T. D., Pham, L. D., Crouch, M., & Springer, M. G. (2020). The correlates of teacher turnover: An updated and expanded meta-analysis of the literature. *Educational Research Review*, *31*, https://doi.org/10.1016/j.edurev.2020.100355

Ronfeldt, M., Loeb, S., & Wyckoff, J. (2013). How teacher turnover harms student achievement. *American Educational Research Journal*, *50*(1), 4–36. https://doi.org/10.3102/0002831212463813

Sutcher, L., Darling-Hammond, L., & Carver-Thomas, D. (2019). Understanding teacher shortages: An analysis of teacher supply and demand in the United States. *Education Policy Analysis Archives*, *27*, 35.

Institute of Educational Sciences School Pulse Data. (2023). U.S. Department of Education, Institute of Education Sciences, National Center for Education Statistics, School Pulse Panel 2021–22, 2022–23, and 2023–24.

Watlington, E., Shockley, R., Guglielmino, P., & Felsher, R. (2010). The high cost of leaving: An analysis of the cost of teacher turnover. *Journal of Education Finance*, *36*(1), 22–37.

Will, M. (2023). *What will teacher shortages look like in 2024 and beyond? A researcher weighs in*. Education Week. https://www.edweek.org/leadership/what-will-teacher-shortages-look-like-in-2024-and-beyond-a-researcher-weighs-in/2023/12

2

Recognize the Need for Change and the Complexities of Change in Practice

Reflecting on the last few years in education may make many education leaders and educators question their career choice. Chapter 1 identified just some of the challenges facing educators, the results of which are reflected in pervasive nationwide educator shortages. How is your school or district navigating the challenges it faces? What is your school/district doing well and what is your vision for the next few years? How are you able to support each other in making small changes that are needed? What about larger system-wide changes that may be necessary?

The purpose of this chapter is to describe how to recognize the need for change and the complexities of change. This chapter provides an overview of the initial process of identifying the status of the school or district and the ways in which this may not match the desired vision. This process of identifying a mismatch between status and desired vision, in other words, recognizing the need for change, is a critical first step in systemic change. This chapter focuses on identifying the specific issues that currently prevent the desired vision or goals from being achieved and offers a process of defining the need. To effect change, organizations should recognize a need for change, gain commitment from all involved and affected by change, and establish a shared vision.

Recognizing the Need for Change

In most cases, recognizing that something needs to change is the impetus for individuals to come together and discuss ways to resolve challenges or needs. Perhaps the need is perfectly clear to some individuals and that is why the organization is looking at how to change and wants to ensure that their efforts will lead to sustainable change. For many school districts and organizations around the world, the pandemic and its aftermath exposed educational, social, and mental health impacts that are still present today (Abrams et al., 2022; Reimers et al., 2022). The pressure to recoup learning losses, accelerate learning, recruit and retain teachers, and address burnout and the mental health of teachers and students in a politically sensitive climate is intense. For teams who have already identified a need, the issue might be which need to prioritize and address first. It is important to consider your organization's current state of being within the context of its strengths and challenges, which includes a review of its organizational culture, the influential environment that surrounds the organization, the infrastructure available to support change, and the commitment to change. This allows the team to reflect upon the full context of their status.

Gaining Commitment for Change

If the leadership is new or the team is uncertain about the concerns of other members of the organization, one option for gathering information about the sense of community or school climate can be to do a brief barometer evaluation or pulse survey with questions adapted for each audience (Huber & Helm, 2020). Partners across the community including teachers, staff, students, parents, and community members can provide input on what is working well, where improvement is

TABLE 2.1 Sample Pulse Survey Questions

Category	Sample Questions
Mission	Are you familiar with our school/district's mission, vision, and goals?
Leadership	Are your school/district's leadership visible and accessible? Do you think the school/district leadership care about you as a person?
Experience	Would you recommend the school/district to friends?
Work/life balance	Does the school/district care about your workplace/mental/physical well-being?
Climate/Engagement	Do you feel accepted and respected here? Are you comfortable contributing your opinions?
Academics	Are all children's academic strengths and challenges appropriately addressed?

Adapted from https://blog.empuls.io/employee-engagement-software/

warranted, and one thing they believe can improve the quality of education or services provided by answering questions such as those in Table 2.1. These data provide some ideas of where the larger community is in terms of what is important and how well-informed they are. The barometer/pulse survey can also serve as a relatively simple ongoing progress monitoring of any strategy implementation (Aderet-German & Ben-Peretz, 2020). If kept simple, perhaps one can use a Google form attached to a text message so participants can check a rating scale once a quarter or once a semester and submit it for consideration. The data can be shared and discussed with the respective partners with appropriate problem-solving or celebrating as needed. Other options for gathering needs assessment data are explored in more detail in Chapter 5.

Developing a Shared Vision

Upon gaining data through the pulse survey, team members can engage in creating a T-Chart to identify strengths and opportunities (Tables 2.2 and 2.3). Then, the team can review the list and identify which opportunities they would like to pursue further and perhaps collect more data to identify the root cause of the issue.

TABLE 2.2 Sample T-Chart

Strengths	Opportunities
Engaged and active parent organization	Some staff shortages (long-term subs)
Seasoned faculty and staff	Some challenges in hiring subs on Fridays
Pretty good facilities	Some persistent behavior challenges
	Some resulting in lowered academic outcomes

TABLE 2.3 T-Chart Template

Strengths	Opportunities

To identify areas of strength and those to improve, describe the gaps between the current state and the ideal or aspirational state of the school or organization (Bryk et al., 2015). Consider whether desired student outcomes and behaviors are achieved. Beyond simple achievement, are there ways that the school or organization could be doing its multiple tasks and roles more effectively, more efficiently, or more inclusively? Are tasks and roles evenly and equitably distributed? If there is one thing that the pandemic brought into the open and forced educational systems to address, it is the very real nature of teacher, student, and administrator burnout (Fox et al., 2021; Marshall & Pressley, 2023). The investigation into these questions involves looking beyond improving student outcomes to *how* we achieve those student outcomes. The link between school culture and climate, or rather the sense of community that educators and employees perceive, educator/employee well-being, and student outcomes is clear (Karnopp & Walls, 2023; Walter & Fox, 2021).

Consider an elementary school located in the high SES part of a rural county in the mid-Atlantic that is currently doing well academically with improved math and reading scores through the use of literacy and math coaches and increased math and literacy time. However, the principal has noticed that, since the pandemic, behaviors in PK-2 classrooms are very challenging and have resulted in a couple of early retirements, multiple office referrals, and referrals for special education. PK-2 teachers are not happy and have involved the teacher's union and the principal has complained to district administration requesting additional support, including additional paraprofessionals, out-of-school placements, and out-of-district placements for the children with challenging behaviors. Although academic outcomes are still maintained, there are clearly other challenges present here.

Complexities of Change

Identifying problems in schools or organizations can sometimes be challenging for policy reasons because it depends on the values and priorities of those defining the problem (Stone et al., 1989). Remember the elementary school's problem with the behaviors of PK-2 students. This became the problem of the special education director because the school determined that the students all needed special education services or needed to be referred for out-of-school placement. When a problem or concern is identified, often it requires a discussion and negotiation of several issues given that our perceptions of the problem often depend on our proximity to the problem. Those who are involved and closest to the problem area identified experience the challenges much differently than those who are not. For instance, consider the problem area in terms of:

- ♦ The severity and its impact on the individual, the classroom, the school, the organization, or the community.
- ♦ The costs involved in the different solutions to the organization.
- ♦ The risks involved in not solving the problem.

Given the complexities of change and the challenges inherent in implementing change in school systems, we are proposing the use of an open systems approach. The application of an open systems approach leads an organization to consider factors from the beginning to recognize potential challenges and enlist all potential partners to engage in problem-solving. When everyone who is involved in the situation is part of the discussion and the problem-solving, collaborative practical solutions are more likely to emerge (Penuel et al., 2020).

With our previous Elementary School, after sending various supports including a behavior specialist and additional paraprofessionals to provide ongoing behavioral support in the classroom, the Special Education Director of the School District arranged to meet with the principal and relevant faculty to discuss the issues. The Special Education Director indicated that she recognized how challenging behaviors had become with the younger students coming back without any prior opportunities for socialization. However, not only is out-of-district placement very unusual and very restrictive for such young children, but it also barely exists except for the most significantly involved cases, and the costs are prohibitive. In addition, when we look at the children's behaviors, they seem to have quite typical behaviors for 4- and 5-year-olds. For example, behavioral observations and data collection showed that students required multiple redirections to complete tasks and frequently wandered around the room, ignoring the teacher's directions. One group of boys who wandered around the room chatting and playing with toys were ignored and not redirected. Two boys and one girl who talked to each other while they wandered around the room were redirected multiple times and were labeled "incorrigible". One strategy the special education director suggested teachers might want to try was behavior-specific praise – she modeled a couple of examples using typical behaviors and indicated that this was an evidence-based practice. She then suggested that perhaps this might be a good place to start.

Clarifying the Need for Change

Defining the problem requires the team of partners to first identify and describe the context and what the current state is, as noted earlier. Our schools all exist in different communities – many of which exhibit very different sets of needs that influence performance. In a study examining outlier schools (high-performing schools among resource-challenged communities), researchers found that principals in outlier schools "were attuned to the local culture ... and had a realistic view of their community's challenges but focused on supporting students through a context-sensitive approach that emphasized assets" (Rushing & Pendola, 2023, p. 97). It is important to describe strengths as well as opportunities, so spend time identifying the things that the school does well and include how they do these well. What data sources are needed to support this? An organizational learning approach seeks data from multiple perspectives as well as data that can be closely tied to the target of improvement and those that address proximal goals rather than a focus on distal accountability objectives. It may include formative classroom data, office referral data, attendance data, an environmental scan, stakeholder surveys, and benchmark data. In considering sources of data for defining the problem and then making decisions, go beyond test scores and student performance data and collect those that may contextualize performance data such as homelessness, special designations, and health (Press Mandinach & Schildman, 2021).

An open systems approach facilitates a fuller understanding of the context in which the school or organization works and the different structures and processes that may support and oppose learning. Research on systems change and organizational learning has led to the emergence of a variety of frameworks and strategies. One of these, the 5 S framework, is shared as one approach to frame and define the problem. Hinnant-Crawford and Anderson (2022) suggest using the 5 S framework for problem definition in improvement-focused education research to address the system strategically and uncover the various sources, root causes, and perspectives of the problem.

This 5 S framework begins by identifying the *Significance* of the problem and the purpose for change. The authors refer to this as what pulls people together (Tables 2.4 and 2.5). The significance should be identified by considering why the problem should be solved, who is impacted, and how alleviating the problem will change lives, experiences, or opportunities. *In our elementary case example, multiple failed attempts to resolve the problem led to a call for school improvement and the principal's decision to take this broader*

TABLE 2.4 Sample 5 S Framework

S-	Definition	In our school...
Significance	Purpose for change, why the problem needs to be solved, and who is impacted.	School population became much more heterogeneous; faculty were unable to meet the needs of students academically and behaviorally and were referring significant numbers of 4- and 5-year-old students for out-of-district placements and for special education
Source	What are the structural, organizational, ideological, capacity, historical, resource, or pedagogical sources of issue?	Structural change in the population, capacity, resources, and pedagogical skills of teachers, administrator, and staff to meet the needs of a more diverse population of students
Substantive focus	What should we prioritize? What should we focus on?	Team decided to focus on additional PD on culturally relevant instruction, motivating and engaging learners with diverse needs, and effective classroom management techniques
Scale	Who will be involved? Define how many, at what level, and to what extent?	Team decided to begin with grades PK-2 and provide PD and coaching on topics indicated earlier
Scope	Where will this take place? Define the depth and breadth of it within the organization	Team indicated that they would scale up to grades 3–5 teachers in year 2

perspective. She brought together a team including some district personnel and community members to review existing school data and they determined that the school personnel needed to become more effective at teaching a more diverse student body. Everyone was impacted and becoming more effective would provide greater opportunities for all their students, not only those recently enrolled because of the opening of a federal prison in the vicinity that had resulted in the relocation of many prisoners' families to the school's catchment area.

The second S refers to the *Source* or what is causing the problem. The source requires the team to think about what structural, organizational, policy, ideological, capacity, historical, resource, or pedagogical sources may be causing the issues. This coincides with the external factors included in the open systems change model – cultural alignment, environmental awareness, and infrastructure support. Look at the issue from multiple perspectives and a user-centered approach. *In our elementary school example, it was clear that the school's population had changed over a previous couple of years from a homogenous upper middle class, white group of children to a more heterogeneous group of students from diverse backgrounds, including risk factors that neither the principal nor teachers were used to teaching.* From teachers' initial frustrations with students and district concerns about teachers' lack of classroom management practices, the teachers were able to come together and identify the malleable source of the problem: the changing needs of the population they were serving. The structural change in their population forced them to review their capacity, resources, and pedagogical skills for teaching a diverse population and facilitated their research into how to engage, motivate, and facilitate effective learning for *all* learners.

Tools that teams can use to establish the Source of a problem, such as Ishikawa's fishbone or the 5 Whys, are further explained in Chapter 5. Once the source is clear, it is time to narrow the focus using the third S, *Substantive focus*. Substantive focus also helps the team to decide what to address in terms of prioritizing what area or issue will be more advantageous to address. *Additional professional development in providing culturally relevant instruction, engaging and motivating learners, and supporting students with diverse needs, in addition to effective classroom management techniques, were all identified as needs by the teachers.* Substantive focus and the final two "Ss" in this framework support the "define the problem" component within the planning cycle of the open systems change model.

As the team defines this problem and states what area they will address, creating a problem statement, they also name the fourth S, the *Scale* of the problem, and define who will be involved. This should include how many, at what level, and to what extent, noting the knowledge and skills needed to solve the problem and carry out any solutions. *The team identified the following as their problem statement: To meet the increasingly diverse needs of students, all teachers, beginning with PK-2 teachers, would participate in ongoing PD and coaching in culturally relevant instruction, engaging and motivating learners and supporting students with diverse needs, and effective classroom management techniques during the school year.* The last step, or last S, involves defining the Scope of the problem, which refers to the location of the problem and the depth and breadth of it within the organization: for example, the classroom, the department, and/or the entire school or district. As indicated earlier, the team elected to begin with grades PK-2 where they believed the problems were most challenging and planned to review the data and then scale up to grades 3-5 the following school year. With the Scale and Scope of their plan identified, the team then continued to plan logistics and resources for professional development and coaching with team members including members from the district administration.

TABLE 2.5 5 S Framework Template

S-	Definition	In our school…
Significance	Purpose for change, why the problem needs to be solved, and who is impacted.	
Source	What are the structural, organizational, ideological, capacity, historical, resource, or pedagogical sources of issue?	
Substantive Focus	What should we prioritize? What should we focus on?	
Scale	Who will be involved? Define how many, at what level, and to what extent?	
Scope	Where will this take place? Define the depth and breadth of it within the organization	

In summary, it is helpful to take an open systems approach and begin by identifying the strengths of the system, including its context and those other influencing factors as well as its opportunities. With partners,

1. Describe the current state of being while considering the culture, environment, and infrastructure.
2. Identify and describe what the ideal looks like for your organization or school and collaboratively establish a shared vision and goal.
3. Identify what is already done to support the shared vision, and
4. Identify what is preventing or hindering the ideal from being.

The hindrances or problems that the team members identify may help clarify the root cause of the problem that the team will address to reach its vision or aspirational state. Once the goal is clearly defined, that is, what it is that needs to change, then the group can identify appropriate data sources for defining both the scope and significance of the problem, researching interventions, as well as evaluating the impact of any changes on it. Chapter 3 describes in more detail the open systems approach and a data-based problem-solving process to achieve change.

We provide change preventers and facilitators in Table 2.6.

TABLE 2.6 Change Preventers and Facilitators

Change Preventers	*Change Facilitators*
Change preventers can include:	Change facilitators can include:
- Focusing solely on strengths or challenges - Not understanding an individual's intentions for change (personal, monetary, passion) and ignoring those intentions - Ignoring proximity of the problem - Responsibility avoidance - Targeting or blaming individuals or groups as the source of a problem (e.g., students, parents)	- Focus on both strengths and challenges - Understanding an individual's intentions for change and asking reflective, strategic, and generative questions - Providing clear roles and responsibilities to individuals based on the problem's proximity and context - Build shared responsibility for challenges and resources acknowledging that areas in need have often been underresourced in the past - Acknowledging that incalcitrant issues need more resources, effective and intensive practices

Reflection Questions

1. Is there recognition for a need for change and who recognizes this need?
2. What is working well, where is improvement warranted, and what is one thing you believe can improve the quality of education or services provided?
3. What are the strengths and opportunities in your team and what gaps do you observe?
4. Identify the 5 Ss from your perspective.

References

Abrams, E. M., Greenhawt, M., Shaker, M., Pinto, A. D., Sinha, I., & Singer, A. (2022). The COVID-19 pandemic: Adverse effects on the social determinants of health in children and families. *Annals of Allergy, Asthma & Immunology*, *128*(1), 19–25.

Aderet-German, T., & Ben-Peretz, M. (2020). Using data on school strengths and weaknesses for school improvement, *Studies in Educational Evaluation*, *64*, 1–9, https://doi.org/10.1016/j.stueduc.2019.100831

Atwood, E. D., Jimerson, J. B., & Holt, B. (2019). Equity-oriented data use: Identifying and addressing food insecurity at Cooper Springs Middle School. *Journal of Cases in Educational Leadership*, *22*(3), 1–16. https://doi.org/10.1177/1555458919859932.

Bryk, A. S., Gomez, L. M., Grunow, A., & LeMahieu, P. G. (2015). *Learning to improve. How America's schools can get better at getting better*. Harvard Education Press.

Fox, H. B., Tuckwiller, E. D., Kutscher, E. L., & Walter, H. L. (2021). What makes teachers well? A mixed methods study of special education teacher well-being. *Journal of Interdisciplinary Studies in Education*, *9*(2), 223–248. https://doi.org/10.32674/jise.v9i2.217

Heumann, J. (2020). *An unrepentant memoir of a disability rights activist*. Beacon.

Hinnant-Crawford, B., & Anderson, E. (2022). 5S framework for problem definition in improvement focused education research. In D. J. Peurach, J. L. Russell, L. Cohen-Vogel, & W. Penuel (Eds.), *The foundational handbook on improvement research in education* (pp. 301–324). Rowman & Littlefield.

Marshall, T. D., & Pressley, T. (2023). *Lessons of the pandemic disruption, innovation, and what schools need to move forward.* Guilford Press.

Penuel, W. R., Riedy, R., Barber, M. S., Peurach, D. J., LeBouef, W. A., & Clark, T. (2020). Principles of collaborative education research with stakeholders: Toward requirements for a new research and development infrastructure. *Review of Educational Research, 90*(5). https://doi.org/10.3102/0034654320938126

Press Mandinach, E., & Schildman, K. (2021). Misconceptions about data-based decision making in education: An exploration of the literature. *Studies in Educational Evaluation, 69,* 1–10, https://doi.org/10.1016/j.stueduc.2020.100842

Prothero, A., & Riser-Kositsky, M. (2022). School counselors and psychologists remain scarce even as needs rise. *Education Week, 41*(24), 3-7.

Reimers, F. M. (2022). Learning from a pandemic. The impact of COVID-19 on education around the world. *Primary and secondary education during Covid-19: Disruptions to educational opportunity during a pandemic,* 1–37.

Rushing, K. J., & Pendola, A. (2023). Outlier leadership in Alabama: Resource challenged schools and principal practices. *Journal of Educational Administration, 61*(2), 89–107. https://doi.org/10.1108/JEA-01-2022-0024

Stone, D. A. (1989). Causal stories and the formation of policy agendas. *Political Science Quarterly, 104*(2), 281–300. https://doi.org/10.2307/2151585

3

The Systems Change Process

In Chapter 2, we discuss the importance of clarifying the need for change. We explored data sources and information that can be used as well as the 5 S framework to specify the problem. In this chapter, we will focus on the change process. That is, once we have clarified the need for change and specified the problem, perhaps through the 5 S process, then the change process can commence.

When you think back on achievements reached and challenges overcome, you can no doubt also identify elements in the environment that served to facilitate your success. By the same token, you may have also experienced elements in the environment that served as barriers. For example, if you were or are an athlete with a particular goal and need to enhance your strength to improve your performance, you likely had access to a practice facility, coaches, or monetary resources to access a facility or coach. What about your educational success? If you had a goal to attain a bachelor's degree and attended post-secondary education with children, you likely had childcare, resources to purchase books and pay for courses, effective instructors, and perhaps a supportive family. With each success we experience, there are resources that fuel our success.

The same is true for our more challenging experiences. If you had a rough semester or academic year, perhaps you were experiencing stressors that did not allow you to give your full attention to your coursework. Perhaps you did not have even one resource to seek additional support with childcare or a course tutor. With each experience we have, there is more than what meets the eye, and each of these contextual elements is like gears on a machine that allows it to either dysfunction or execute effectively.

The same is true for the education landscape. There are a variety of factors that ultimately influence student academic and social outcomes and our ability as leaders to improve these. Educators must consider and attend to all these impacting variables to ensure the education landscape is operating efficiently and effectively with measurable outputs. Various components to consider include governance, finance, personnel, educator practice, educator and workplace well-being, student outcomes, and the community within which we are located. Although it is critical to recognize all the various components that work together to ensure academic and social success, it is not enough to just consider these elements, their functioning, and their influence. It is also imperative that there is an intentional, data-based process in place to ensure they are operating at their optimal level.

Therefore, upon clarifying the need for change discussed in Chapter 2 and considering all the factors that influence outcomes, in this chapter we identify a process that will result in a visible change from identifying partners to conducting a needs assessment to identifying a solution and developing an action plan to implementation support and data-based decision-making. Within each of these chapters, we propose a cyclical process including *(a) reflect, (b) plan, (c) implement, and (d) study* (Table 3.1). Because this is a cyclical and ongoing process, upon engaging in study, the next step is to continue to reflect. This cycle is necessary to ensure teams use a data-based process that results in outcomes, including students' academic and social outcomes. Considering the scenarios previously presented, it was not enough to just have access to resources, and it was not enough to just have childcare available. If either of these scenarios applied to you, you likely easily recognized that there were steps involved to secure these resources and thus experience positive outcomes. Therefore, the purpose of this chapter

TABLE 3.1 Framework Components

Component of Cycle	Definition	Examples of Activities
Reflect	Determine what you will do next based upon data	Based on the data available to team members
Plan	Identifying goals and procedures to achieve goals	The Lars School System determined they wanted to identify community partners to develop a resource bank for families. The school system assigned each team member a resource type to investigate and report back at their next monthly meeting.
Implement	Using the plan to move into practice	Team members researched and contacted community resources aligned with their assignment.
Study	Collect informal and/or formal data	As team members collected information, they made a note of whether the entities they communicated with would be interested in being added to the resource bank.

is to introduce you to the cyclical process that can support leaders in systems change. We revisit this process throughout the chapters within this book to ensure the entities with whom you partner are both efficient and effective.

Reflect takes place when we decide what we are going to do next based upon the information or data that we have available. This information may come from our observations, records, or information that has been shared with us (e.g., pulse check). It entails making a decision with the information we have collected. Reflect is a critical start to the implementation process as it allows us to then use intentionality when engaging in the next step, plan.

The *plan* component of the cycle includes identifying the goal and clarifying the steps to get there. Without a plan, particularly when a team is working with many partners (e.g., teachers, administrators, families), it is impossible to experience outcomes. Consider the athletic or academic experiences previously mentioned. There had to be a plan related to what resources would be accessed, how they would be accessed, when they would be accessed, and who would access them. Otherwise, they were just good ideas that went no further.

Next is *implement, which* is moving the plan into practice. This can often be where teams get stuck. Hence why we believe this cycle is critical for teams to be both efficient and effective in achieving their goals ultimately to enhance student academic and social outcomes. Once a plan is developed, it is time to move the plan into implementation. The plan should specify things like who, when, and how to support and facilitate implementation. In other words, during implement, the team is doing the actions from the plan component. In the athletic and academic example, once a plan was developed of who, what, how, and when, it was time to move into implementation. For those who identified and planned how to access the athletic resources, they could then move those ideas into implementation. Others potentially identified resources and created a plan to consume childcare and secured resources to pay for courses and books. Those plans needed to be moved into implementation to experience the athletic and academic outcomes.

Next, *study* entails collecting data, analyzing the data, and evaluating the data. Collecting data may be either informal or formal or both informal and formal. For example, the athlete driving to the coaching facility each day may informally take data on the amount of time they are spending driving, yet also notice the outcomes they are experiencing in their athletic performance. The same is true for the academic who perhaps is investing in childcare but noticing there is dedicated, uninterrupted study time. In both the athletic and academic examples, formal data collection could also occur. For example, in the athletic example, the individual could chart their progress using a mobile application such as "Lose It". In the academic example, the student could monitor how much time they are spending studying and chart their grades using a system such as Google Forms. In study both informal and formal data can be collected to engage in data-based decision-making. Upon study, we continue to engage in the cycle with reflect. Once teams make a

TABLE 3.2 Change Preventers and Facilitators

Change Preventers	Change Facilitators
Change preventers can include:	Change facilitators can include:
- Disagreements regarding the goal, the process, roles or the data - Not knowing enough background history to accurately reflect	- Spend time building relationships to have a better understanding of team members and the expertise they bring to the team - Bringing team members along in the history and context of the school for intentional decision-making

decision, it is time to plan, then implement and study, and reflect. It is an ongoing cycle. We will revisit what this cycle might look like in practice within each of the following chapters.

As you consider the cyclical process of reflect, plan, implement, and study, you may face change preventers and facilitators. We have identified some examples of preventers and facilitators to overcome these challenges in Table 3.2.

Reflection Questions

1. What are the experiences you have with reflect, plan, study, and implement?
2. Where do you anticipate teams might be most likely to get "stuck" in this process?
3. How might teams overcome setbacks within the reflect, plan, study, and implement cycle?

4

Collaboration and How It Connects with the System

Chapter 3 presented information about the steps we believe will result in visible and sustainable change through a cyclical process including: *(a) reflect, (b) plan, (c) implement, and (d) study.* This cycle is necessary to ensure teams use a data-based process that results in outcomes. This chapter will focus specifically on collaboration and strategies you can choose from while working with different partners in unique, context-specific systems.

An Interconnected System

We all have experience with the ebbs and flows of weather and how it influences us as individuals, communities, and societies. Weather works within systems (both internal and external). Long-term climate changes can directly and indirectly affect many aspects of society in potentially positive or negative ways, as an adequate amount of rainfall helps the earth, plants, water source, and air, while increasing warmer temperatures could increase air conditioning costs and could affect the spread of diseases and air quality (breathing) but could have some positive effects on crops. More frequent and intense weather changes can affect vulnerable populations and damage environments in ways that are hard to predict or reverse. Weather is a concrete example we can use to help us understand the intricacies of collaboration within a system. Just like weather influences our world in different ways, the ways in which we engage and interact with others can also influence how we react to different situations or stimuli in our environment.

Collaboration

While collaboration can be defined in many ways, all types of collaboration involve intricate practices involving trust, communication, and respect for true innovation to occur. We are all complex individuals who bring our understanding, knowledge, experiences, and identities to a problem of practice as we work together to create impact. At its core, collaboration occurs when we are more than the sum of our parts (Birney et al., 2019). In this book, we are using a definition that moves beyond a process-oriented definition to leveraging collective intelligence and garnering multiple perspectives together for a larger purpose other than oneself, which shapes the ecosystem of which you are a part (just like the weather system) (Collaborations, 2022). In education, collaboration can happen within your field of study or discipline or outside your field. For example, as a district leader or superintendent, you can work with policymakers or lawyers. As an educator, you partner with families and may also collaborate with psychologists, social workers, or occupational therapists to support students in your classroom. Collaborating outside of your field can be called interdisciplinary, interagency, or multi-disciplinary collaboration. Collaborating inside and outside of your field has many costs and benefits, such as having too similar perspectives that do not allow you to generate new and innovative solutions, or if you do work with outside collaborators, it may be hard to identify a common goal. In essence, collaboration is a complex system that helps shape decisions.

For collaboration to occur, trust must be established. A major obstacle to building trust, fostering collaboration, and creating innovation is a form of resistance called *masquerading*. Individuals within a group (often leaders) who avoid confrontation (often presented as trust), such as showing up on time for meetings and listening intently, as well as offering brainstorming sessions that are equated with innovation, may be initially seen as collaborative approaches but are often practices that may reflect a further masquerade, resistant for fear of change, or simply an honest lack of understanding of the rigors of innovation at top management levels. Avoiding confrontation and agreeing with all team members almost always ends in a worse place than where you left off. If you have ever taken courses in attachment theory, you know that an individual's ability to manage stress and maintain emotional stability is rooted in the idea of a secure base (or someone you trust). Trust is acquired through repeated interactions with responsive attachment figures. Therefore, when weathering a storm or when in need of support, the people who reside in your secure base typically remain stable, responsive, and supportive, which enables you to be emotionally available to receive that support (Mikulincer & Shaver, 2023). In the workplace, trust is established through feeling as though one has a voice, and one is heard. This should not be confused with agreement, but rather there is an environment in which team members can engage in mutual exchanges of information and each team member feels they have a voice and are heard. Collaboration is multi-faceted and is built upon trust, respecting differing perspectives, and working together toward a purpose larger than yourself.

Reflect

The key foundations of building sustainable systems incorporate (1) fostering connection, (2) embracing context, and (3) reconfiguration of power (Rayner & Bonnici, 2021). Therefore, cultivating collaborative systems requires reflection at all steps (i.e., create connection, trust, and opportunities for all voices to be heard). Collaboration is the foundation of the "So what" of systems change and often the primary reason implementation and sustainability do not see daylight. Understanding individual personalities and profiles and focusing those individuals' passions in a way that can drive change for that specific program of practice can help increase trust, a sense of belonging and shared ownership to the work, and a shift in power from authoritative to collaborative which drives effective sustainable change. There are also examples of what collaboration is not, and usually these are not explicit (outwardly noticeable) but implicit (subtle) and almost always toxic. Toxic environments are ones in which you feel as though the workload is too high, you have no control or agency in decision-making, and there is no clarity on your roles and how you will get ahead within your job. It is important to understand and recognize noncollaborative efforts so that you can set boundaries, attempt to build trust, and frame questions that will open space for discussion and growth. As a first step, it is important to reflect upon the collaborations that are in place or the collaborations that may need to be built. For those that are in place, what is the health of those collaborations? Do team members engage with one another? Do they share new ideas? Is there an environment of mutual respect and understanding? Where is collaboration needed? Reflecting upon your collaboration skills can also provide insight to how you currently are or might consider contributing to teams. You can use the individual assessment to help you become more aware of your collaboration style (Table 4.1).

Plan

Fostering Connection: Embracing Multiple Perspectives

Once teams have reflected upon the collaborations that are in place or the collaborations that might need to be built, it is important to plan for effective collaboration. Planning for effective collaboration is centered on understanding the perspectives, experiences, and unique expertise of those you will be or are collaborating with. When leaders can identify why team members are passionate about certain topics or choose or request to participate in certain initiatives, it can help in understanding effective collaboration strategies, such as leveraging one's strengths. Understanding different team members' perspectives, experiences, and unique

TABLE 4.1 Collaboration Skills – Individual Self Checklist

Activity	Rating 1–3 1–Regularly 2–Sometimes 3–Needs work	How can I improve in this area?
I am respectful even with people that I disagree with.		
I maintain a positive attitude when working as part of a group.		
I am fully engaged with the group and contribute willingly.		
I accept responsibility (volunteer) for tasks that need to be accomplished.		
I enjoy serving in a leadership role.		
I am good at active listening and allow others to speak and contribute equally.		
I work well with others. Even those are different from myself.		
I am comfortable giving team members constructive feedback.		
I complete tasks on time.		
I stay focused and remain on task.		
I try to find time to meet with the team.		

strengths can also support teams to engage effectively with one another. With this understanding, team members can ensure that everyone feels respected as a member of the team. This information can be gathered by identifying individual perspectives based on conversations and observations. Additionally, you can provide a short survey or questionnaire to understand team members' reason for wanting to contribute to the team and the expertise and experience they bring. Gathering this information and pairing their responses with your observations allows teams to determine team members' perspectives, expertise, experiences, and passions, which in turn will be helpful in considering team members' strengths and interests and thus roles and

TABLE 4.2 Interview Questions

Interview Question	Response
Why are you interested in serving on this team?	"I want to serve on this committee because I have seen from experience that my children are not benefiting from the current math curriculum".
How do you view the role of a team member?	"I view my job as to share my experiences and provide insight into how the parent community is thinking".
What skills, expertise and perspectives could you bring to the team?	"I think I could bring my skills in coaching because I work with companies to help improve job performance".
Describe a time when you went above and beyond your duties to help a team reach its goal?	"One time the chair of the committee was sick, and I took over their role for a month".
How should a team member balance transparency and confidentiality?	"You should always be clear and honest especially when deciding on an issue, but never telling the community what is said in meetings and how individuals arrived at a decision".
How would you describe your communication style?	"I have a more dominant personality and like to ask questions other people are not asking".
How do you handle stress or pressure?	"I work in many different companies with many different personalities and handle stress easily".
What motivates you?	"Helping to support my kids and their academic outcomes".
How do you promote diversity, equity and inclusion in teamwork?	"There should be diversity in age, gender, race, ethnicity, and ability on committees".
How would you approach risk-assessments in decision-making?	"As a team"
What do you see as emerging trends in [topic] in education?	"That students are not learning math at the levels they should be, and I would like to help support that effort".

responsibilities within a team. Table 4.2 provides some examples of information you might gather, and Table 4.3 provides a template for teams to adapt and use as appropriate.

Teams might also consider gathering information regarding team member profiles to help them understand the perspectives,

TABLE 4.3 Interview Questions – Blank Form

Interview Question	Response
Why are you interested in serving on this team?	
How do you view the role of a team member?	
What skills, expertise and perspectives could you bring to the team?	
Describe a time when you went above and beyond your duties to help a team reach its goal?	
How should a team member balance transparency and confidentiality?	
How would you describe your communication style?	
How do you handle stress or pressure?	
What motivates you?	
How do you promote diversity, equity and inclusion in teamwork and in teamwork?	
How would you approach risk-assessments in decision-making?	
What do you see as emerging trends in [topic] in education?	

opinions, lenses, and foci that different team members have. This will provide teams with information regarding where team members are coming from as it relates to their opinions and perspectives, which can help with gaining more understanding regarding team members (Table 4.4).

Embracing Contexts: Cultivating Strengths on Your Team

Taking on a leadership position is no easy task. Building a successful team increases productivity and efficiency, increases retention and satisfaction, supports team members in leveraging their strengths, and improves decision-making and long-term sustainability. Understanding team members leadership style and how this may be different from others can also be helpful information to share with teams as it provides team members the opportunity to gain understanding regarding the unique strengths each team member brings as it relates to their leadership style. Figure 4.1 provides an example of leadership styles,

TABLE 4.4 Profiles of a Committee Member – Adapted from NAIS, Profiles of a Board Member

Committee: Curriculum Committee
School: BeachFront School

Team Member 1	Team Member 2	Team Member 3
Jonathan is an instructional coach who has specific ideas and expectations about the implementation of curriculum that conflict with the current reality of the school and its population as his children go to the school and he is deeply invested in the outcomes of his children. His main decision-making drivers focus on ensuring that the "school gets back on track to academic success".	Alejandra is an early intervention classroom teacher with specific skill sets (knowledge and experience) who can assist in the identification of adapting curriculum for children with differing needs. She is interested in being on this committee to grow her practice, contribute to change, and expand her reputation, knowledge, and expertise.	Isabella is an assistant principal who has personal connections to the school as she went there as a child and has lived in the neighborhood her whole life. She feels that the school and its community have contributed to her success, and she wants to be a part of its growth by supporting the curricular decisions and needs moving forward.
Jonathan's lens is focused on *his* children's outcomes	Alejandra's lens is twofold: (1) bringing her knowledge and expertise and (2) expanding her practice and reputation	Isabella's lens is connection to community and the sustainability of traditions plus innovation

01	Democratic Leader	• Decisions are based on input from others • Support team in cultivating strengths • Make sure decisions are made timely
02	Strategic Leader	• Decisions are based on strategy and goals • Decisions are made fast and are connected to goals • Make sure to include others in the process
03	Coaching Leader	• Decisions are based on enhancing strengths to increase collaboration • Supports individual strengths • Make sure to focus on actionable goals
04	Bureaucratic Leader	• Decisions come from policy or supervisor • Values decisions made and works within guidelines • Make sure to leverage creative voices on your team
05	Transformational Leader	• Decisions are based on thinking in new ways • Supports creativity and innovation • Make sure to leverage strategic thinkers

FIGURE 4.1 Leadership styles: Strengths and needs

their definitions, strengths of each style, and what leaders need to reflect upon as they plan to collaborate with their team.

Implement

After you can understand team members' experiences, unique expertise, lens, perspectives, and leadership style, you are better equipped to cultivate a collaborative working group. This is because you not only know about your strengths and opportunities for growth, but you also can more easily reflect on how to support others in cultivating their strengths to increase productivity. Two specific strategies one can use to help increase collaboration using strategies from coaching and democratic and strategic leadership that can help build a cohesive team are implementing framing strategies and shared expectations.

Reconfiguration of Power: The Framing Strategy

One specific strategy that can be used to build trust and rapport as well as increase respect for differing perspectives is called *framing*. As leaders, you can frame questions and responses based on different personalities. Just like we differentiate questions for children, we can differentiate the way we ask questions to adults in meetings, based on their needs to ensure each team member feels heard and has a voice in the process and decisions being made as well as meeting team members where they are and pushing them to reflect further. In Table 4.5, you can see how you can effectively shift the tone from reactive to proactive and responsive while acknowledging the committee members' concerns and passion to an actionable step.

Reconfiguration of Power: Creating Shared Expectations

Creating expectations for team members to effectively collaborate is critical. All team members should be engaged and have a voice in what expectations and cultural norms are important for the team. This supports individuality and conformity as well as diversity and inclusion. Team members that have shared expectations have guidelines and boundaries to their

TABLE 4.5 Framing Questions in Meetings (Adapted from NAIS, Profiles of a Board Member)

Discussion Topic: Are the mandated kindergarten state standards "developmentally appropriate" for all children including children with disabilities and English Language Learners? Are we using both Developmentally Appropriate Practices (DAP; NAEYC) and Recommended Practices (DEC) to adapt curriculum to support children in meeting those standards?

Team Member	Committee Member Statement	Leader Framing
Team Member 1–Jonathan	"My daughter has been struggling with writing all year and there has been no support. What resources are we even using?"	"I am wondering how many students are struggling in writing, and what standards are specifically challenging. Do you think we can get that data? Would you be able to lead this process for the next meeting?"
Team Member 2–Alejandra	"Every few years they increase the level of the standards. Kindergarten is the new first grade. It's exhausting. There are children with and without disabilities coming into school who are unable to read (as they should) and the standards really expect you to come in as a reader because you must go through the curriculum so fast".	"This is a point of contention that has been discussed in the education field for some time. Alejandra, you are on the regional Division of Early Childhood board, is that correct? Are there initiatives or resources you could provide that would help us think through some of these critical issues?"
Team Member 3–Isabella	"I honestly do not think we have a problem. We have had standards for decades. I went to school here and succeeded. I was a teacher here and now a VP and while we make adaptations, the foundation of what we teach needs to stay the same. We do not want to change our mission of academic success".	"There are great models to learn and grow from here as the school has been within this community for a long time. I am wondering if you could work with Jonathan to identify the specific data on writing and figure out where the gaps are so we can come discuss this next meeting?"

work together, which creates structure, a respect for workplace and individual well-being, and trust. Creating shared expectations that align to the mission and goals of the work can help reduce the impact of interpersonal conflicts and increase shared decision-making. When everyone understands the direction of the work, the team can work more effectively. Statements you can use as you go through this process should be stated in positive language and be clear and concise. Some examples include: "We accomplish tasks on time", "We actively listen and respond to others", and "We coordinate meetings at times that respect all members". Additionally, there can be statements on inclusivity, diversity, and equity such as "We respect others even when we disagree" and "We adapt and accommodate to individual differences when needed".

Study

Upon engaging in reflect, plan, and implement, teams should engage in study, which allows them to assess the collaborative health of their teams. Ample research states that individuals do not fully understand the job roles and responsibilities of others in their field. It would be hard as they do not experience the day-to-day job duties as one would if they were performing the tasks. For example, administrators and educators often state that they are frustrated that the other does not understand the role they play, and decisions made are often taken personally, which increases negative workplace culture, ineffective communication, and lower effectiveness. To offset this and to build a bridge between these job role experiences and perspectives, one must understand the barriers to success and opportunities for growth so that team members can leverage strengths to accomplish goals. The Self-assessment for Collaborative Teams in Table 4.6 can help teams assess and strengthen collaboration.

Adapted from New Jersey Collaborative Teams ToolKit Foundational Self-Assessment downloaded June 14, 2024, from https://www.nj.gov/education/AchieveNJ/teams/SelfAssessment.pd

TABLE 4.6 Self-Assessment for Collaborative Teams

Instructions: Using the scale below, rate and describe your current practices and planning time for collaborative teams.

Time for Collaboration

4	3	2	1	Other Comments
We have regular collaborative planning time daily or weekly, built in as part of the school schedule.	We have collaborative planning time occasionally (monthly or less) over the course of the school year.	We have collaborative planning time infrequently (PD days) or outside of the school day.	We do not have collaborative planning time.	

Adequate Materials and Resources

4	3	2	1	Other Comments
Our team has access to all necessary materials and resources.	Our team has access to some materials and/or resources and knows how to request additional from the school.	Our team has access to some materials and/or resources but does not have a way to request additional from the school.	Our team does not have access to any necessary materials or resources.	

Clear Articulated Roles and Responsibilities (e.g., team leader, facilitator, notetaker ...)

4	3	2	1	Other Comments
Our team has a clearly established structure with defined functions, and staff play these roles effectively.	Our team has a clearly established structure with defined functions, but staff does not participate and/or fulfill these roles consistently.	Team members have informal roles and expectations are unclear for how staff should participate or fulfill these roles.	Team members do not have clearly defined roles.	

(Continued)

TABLE 4.6 (Continued)

		Shared Vision and Goals		
4	3	2	1	Other Comments
All participating staff have a shared vision for how collaboration supports improving problems of practice and overall well-being and can articulate a set of clear goals that will help them achieve this vision.	Most participating staff have a shared vision for how collaboration supports improving problems of practice and overall well-being but less can articulate a set of clear goals that will help them achieve this vision.	Less than half of participating staff have a shared vision of how collaboration supports improving problems of practice and overall well-being and there is little consensus around how this vision translates into goals.	There is little to no shared vision of how collaboration supports improving problems of practice and overall well-being.	

If you identified any items in 1, 2, or 3, you may want to use the Building Collaborative Teams Action Plan (Table 4.7) to focus your team's efforts on supporting shared decision-making and increased collaboration, which will help establish a foundation for the work ahead.

TABLE 4.7 Building Collaborative Teams – Action Plan

Directions: Based on your Self-Assessment for Collaborative Teams, identify next steps for how you will support building your team or the adjustments you will make within your current collaborative team structure and a timeline for doing this.

Next Steps	Intended Outcome	Timeline

TABLE 4.8 Change Preventers and Facilitators

Change Preventers	Change Facilitators
Change preventers can include: - Focusing solely on challenges or issues - Targeting individuals or groups as challenge areas without identifying responsible for (victim-blaming – either students or teachers or parents for long-standing challenges) - Thinking that everyone is hearing the same message	Change facilitators can include: - Build relationships and shared responsibility among diverse members of the collaborative team - Focus on the unique strengths that each member brings to the team and how that helps to both see the big picture and identify resources and solutions that embrace the whole community/district/school - Check in frequently with the team to ensure that team members have the same understanding of the vision. Communication of the message is not always as consistent as one thinks.

Conclusion

Collaboration is hard work, and the ability to cultivate trust, build a positive culture, and support multiple perspectives to make decision-making processes that everyone feels comfortable with and a part of is extremely challenging, but critical to sustainable change. To engage in effective collaboration resulting in efficient and productive outcomes, it is important to focus on the "sum of all its parts". Table 4.8 includes change preventers and facilitators teams may experience as they engage in collaboration.

Reflection Questions

1. With whom do you collaborate?
2. What are the perspectives of those you collaborate?
3. How does your team leverage the unique expertise and lens of each team member?
4. What are your team's shared expectations?

References

Birney, A., Cubista, J, Thornton-Papi, D., Winn, L. (2019). Systems change education in innovative contexts: Report and Reflections. Catalyst 2030. https://systemschangeeducation.com/report

Mikulincer, M., & Shaver, P. R. (2023). *Attachment theory expanded.* Guilford Publications.

Rayner. C., & Bonnici, F. (2021). *The Systems Work of Social Change: How to Harness Connection, Context, and Power to Cultivate Deep and Enduring Change.* Oxford University Press

5

Data-Based Needs

In Chapter 4, we discussed the necessity of collaboration to engage all team members through an interconnected system that focuses on (1) fostering connection, (2) embracing context, and (3) reconfiguration of power (Rayner & Bonnici, 2021). The focus of this chapter is to address considerations as teams conduct a needs assessment. A needs assessment is a systematic process for understanding current strengths or gaps within an organization that helps to understand strengths, weaknesses, opportunities, and threats (SWOT) within the organization. We will continue to use our *(a) reflect, (b) plan, (c) implement, and (d) study* process as we discuss conducting a needs assessment. A needs assessment includes five steps: (1) *explore* (explore and identify the problem; SWOT analysis); (2) *collect* (collect holistic data sets); (3) *interpret* (interpret and synthesize findings); (4) *confirm* (conduct a root cause analysis and confirm identified problem); and (5) *draw conclusions and recommendations* (prepare summary of findings, action plan, and dissemination).

What Is a Needs Assessment?

After losing many talented educators and staff last year, even some that have been working in the school for more than five years. Dr. Johnson, a Principal of a Title I high school, was committed to understanding how to attract and retain staff in his high school. He knows that working in a Title I alternative high school is challenging, but he was determined to understand what the factors were that led to this mass exit. He considered the team members who would have relevant and valuable information to share related to this dilemma. This included teachers, families, instructional assistants, other administrators, and students. He began to think about what types of information would be helpful to gain a deeper understanding of factors leading to the mass exit. He recognized that there may be needs as well as strengths that other team members could help him identify. He began to consider how he might best capture this information. He thought about surveys, interviews, and focus groups. He thought about the questions he might include to ensure all the team members had the opportunity to share their unique perspectives and experiences.

Many leaders and educators face dilemmas like Dr. Johnson. A needs assessment is defined as a systematic process for understanding current strengths or gaps within an organization. This process is dynamic and multi-dimensional and grounded in context (individual and contextual needs; Walter et al., 2024). Just like air traffic controllers or crossing guards, individuals in the organization are addressing many macro- and micro-level decisions daily. Implementing a needs assessment can provide a more nuanced understanding of the organization's specific needs that set up a strong foundation for the organization's culture, staff, students, and families.

Reflect

A first step is for leaders to reflect upon the workplace context. Leaders might consider the *pulse check* we discussed in Chapter 2, which provides a sense of the workplace climate. Leaders can also reflect upon their existing data, such as enrollment, achievement, progress monitoring, attendance, and office referral data using the 5 S framework (see Chapter 2) to analyze what they think is the root cause or the aspects they believe they must gain additional information to propel their team forward. We recognize the workplace is a complex and intricate system that is composed of diverse individuals, perspectives, and goals that keep the system running. This presents the opportunity to reflect upon your team culture. Teams might reflect upon, "What is the first aspect of our climate we need to address before anything else can be achieved". Some examples might include relationship building, trust building, mission clarity, and identity and equity awareness such as race, culture, ethnicity, gender, and ability differences.

Second, leaders might consider identifying the possible gaps the organization may have. To identify these gaps, teams can conduct strengths, weaknesses, opportunities, and threats (SWOT) analysis. A SWOT analysis's primary purpose is to help develop awareness of all factors that could be involved in deciding the next step. While the main objective of this tool is to understand gaps or challenges, it is important to highlight and leverage strengths. A SWOT analysis involves making lists (strengths, weaknesses, threats, and opportunities) within a grid with one square for each of the four aspects (strengths, weaknesses, opportunities, and threats). Each grid states a question you pose as a team (Tables 5.1 and 5.2). Last, the team will compare these lists side by side and your team will notice connection or disconnection to discuss more in depth.

TABLE 5.1 SWOT Analysis Example

Strengths	Weaknesses
What is our strongest asset?	What expertise do we lack?
Opportunities	Threats
What are the current trends in this topic area?	Are there any changing funding streams, policies, or laws that will affect decisions?

TABLE 5.2 SWOT Template

Strengths	Weaknesses
Opportunities	Threats

Data-Based Needs ◆ 45

Another strategy teams can consider using to reflect upon the challenges and strengths of a focus topic is the fishbone diagram. This can be done in combination or separately from a SWOT analysis as they both help identify gaps and strengths within your organization. A fishbone diagram is a visual representation of a problem (Desai et al., 2015). This allows teams to diagnose problems instead of targeting symptoms of those problems, which helps teams to move beyond challenges to uncover the root cause of the problem. A fishbone diagram takes its name from its shape (see later). Traditionally, fishbone diagrams focused solely on the barriers to organizations, but we propose that barriers and facilitators must be identified to use the organization's strengths to support continuous improvement (see Figures 5.1-5.3; Walter et al., 2024). The first example shows barriers with a focus topic of optimizing well-being and increasing teacher retention with different proposed ideas for barriers on the fishbones.

A SWOT analysis and/or Fishbone diagram can support the needs assessment processes by incorporating contextualized questions with all team members' voices and experiences. Evidence indicates that teams that cultivate diversity across ethnicity, race, gender, ability, socioeconomic status, religion, sexual orientation, ability, and professional expertise increase

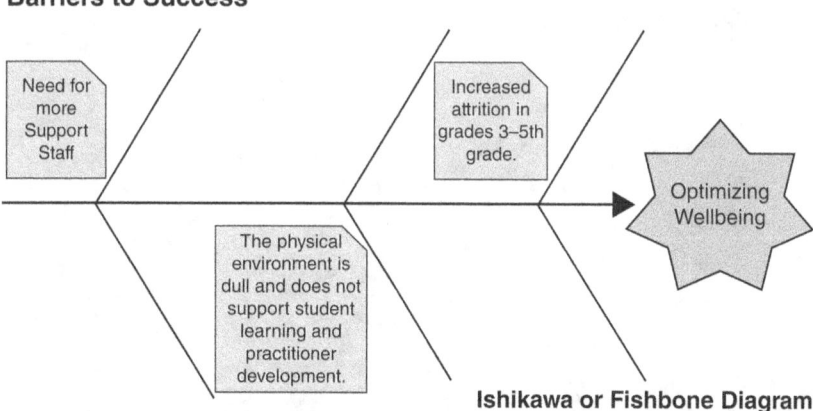

FIGURE 5.1 Example: Fishbone diagram barriers

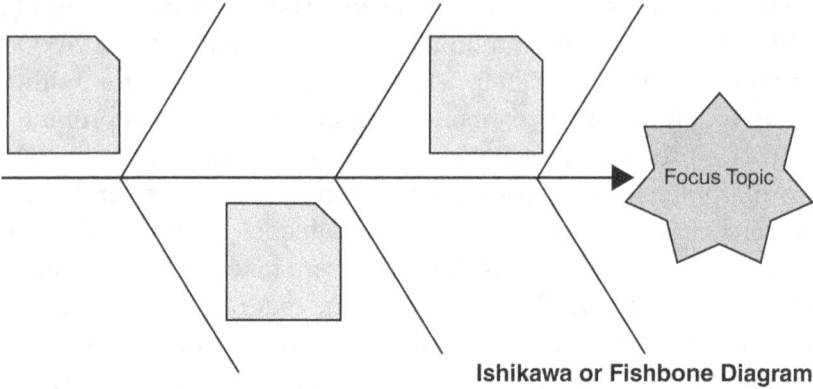

FIGURE 5.2 Fishbone diagram for SWOT analysis: Barriers to success cited in Walter et al., (2024)

work productivity, innovation, and impact. Conversations that include diversity of perspectives and a culture that embraces healthy agreements and disagreements come to understand the organization's needs more clearly. Research also indicates that when employees are in a safe, supportive environment, they will feel more comfortable voicing their opinions, needs, and wants. Therefore, when going through the *reflect* phase of the process, the goal is to foster new ideas in a way that allows all

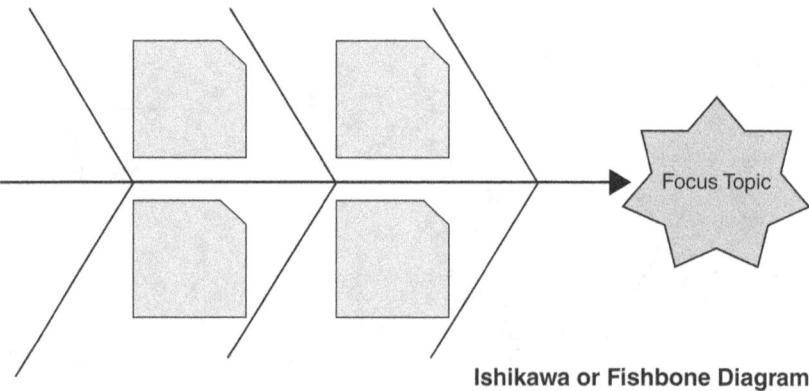

FIGURE 5.3 Fishbone diagram for SWOT analysis: Facilitators to success cited in Walter et al., 2024

employees to be advocates of their own growth (Banerjee & Luckner, 2014; Walter et al., 2024). While all individuals cannot work on the needs assessment, as large groups working on one document is often challenging, giving voice to all team members is critical to impact and innovation. For example, leaders should reflect upon how they can incorporate employee voice such as preferences, interests, challenges, and strengths to understand what employees want and need to support their professional growth and personal well-being as they gather information for a long-term roadmap. Together, these strategies will help support the identification of the primary gaps and organizational strengths so that the team can move from identification through each component of the systematic processes to plan for making data-informed decisions.

Plan

In the planning phase, leaders can use the information they gathered from the SWOT analysis, pulse check, and/or fishbone diagram to help inform what additional data they need. The questions leaders ask allow insights into how to develop recommendations and practices that are culturally sensitive, contextually relevant, and highly effective at addressing the root cause of the problem rather than just looking at the symptoms. For example, if the SWOT analysis suggested the root cause was well-being and retention, leaders can plan to ask questions about (1) opinions, such as "what do team/leaders believe could impact and optimize well-being and increase retention?", (2) solutions, such as "what would the solved or acceptable solution look like?", and (3) organizational priorities and practices, such as "how committed is the leader/team to using the results of the needs assessment to inform planning decisions?" These questions can help take a deep dive into specific questions needed to answer the specific focus topic (e.g., optimizing well-being and increasing retention).

Second, teams can use the information gathered to select potential additional data sources. To do this, the team can identify

(1) what literature, reports, articles, or media coverage provide insight into the questions you are asking (e.g., what are national retention rates for special education teachers?), (2) are there existing needs assessments that address similar topics, have you done this work before?, (3) who might hold information/what voices may not be accounted for that may not be reported or published?, (4) what data do you have that is already collected and analyzed that can be used to understand the priority topic?, this is called secondary data, and (5) what data do you need to collect and how can you diversify the measurements (surveys) and research methods (i.e., quantitative, survey vs. qualitative, focus groups) you use to gain a holistic understanding of the focus topic? For example, if your focus topic is related to increasing well-being at the school level, the team needs to think about what measurements to use and multiple outcome tools can capture the focus topic you identified. It can be beneficial to use multiple sources of data to provide a holistic picture (Fox et al., 2023). Here is one way you can use these questions in the form of a checklist to help plan for gathering data (Table 5.3).

Third, selecting surveys (quantitative) that align with your questions and creating interviews or focus groups (qualitative) that align with the focus topic can provide insightful information. Starting with surveys to gather initial data with follow-up

TABLE 5.3 Checklist for Data Collection Methods

Question	Yes or no
Have you been able to access existing data at local and school levels?	
Have you gathered a range of data across several academic, social-emotional outcomes, or workplace well-being (i.e., retention of educators)?	
Are there any areas where there is little or no data? Does it exist? How would you obtain this data?	
Do you have a balance of quantitative or qualitative data?	
Have you collected data on target populations?	
Have you collected data across schools or organizations?	
What voices are present and what voices are missing?	

focus groups can provide richer information than only doing a survey. A focus group allows teams to dig deeper into the responses that emerged within the survey. There are also formal, validated measures that teams might consider depending upon the topic(s) that emerge within their needs assessment. Specific measurement tools that can be used for looking at school-based well-being and retention in combination with qualitative data include: (1) general and subjective well-being (Positive and Negative Affect Scale; Flourishing Scale; Diener et al., 2009), (2) specific teacher well-being (Teacher Subjective Well Being Questionnaire; Renshaw et al., 2015), and (3) the school climate (School Organizational Health Questionnaire; Hart et al., 2000). These scales ask employees to rate their feelings on their perceptions of going to work, what work increases well-being and what increases burnout, and their perceptions on school morale. When using these in combination with open-ended questions, interviews, or focus groups, you can highlight overall climate profiles and targeted experiences with examples. You are also able to see if the data is similar or different as well as other patterns that emerge that are important for analysis and context-specific recommendations. When teams see common themes emerge across data sources, they can be more confident in their results as similar patterns have emerged across sources. In summary, picking scales that most closely align with the focus topic and designing qualitative questions that align with your focus topic are critical to getting the answers you are seeking. We have included one sample question leaders might consider related to various topics to include in a needs assessment (see Table 5.4).

Planning for data collection and analysis is critical as the methods you pick drive results and implementation. Data collection and analysis should involve a smaller group of individuals (administrators or outside consultants) who can maintain confidentiality and objectivity and who can provide general themes and not individual participant scores. Confidentiality in data collection and reporting enhances representation of diverse populations within the team you are collaborating with and the overall educational organization. This in turn establishes trust and empowers all voices in

TABLE 5.4 Sample Questions Related to Teacher Well Being and Retention

Topic: Optimize Teacher Well-being and Increase Teacher Retention	
Question: Are teachers experiencing burnout due to school-related factors (administration, paperwork, challenging behaviors)?	Method - Quantitative Survey (TSWQ, Diener et al., 2009) - Qualitative: Focus Groups Sources - Attrition and retention interviews and school culture surveys
Question: Are administrators fostering positive connections with teachers in schools?	Method - Qualitative Interviews Sources - Administrator and teacher relationships and perceptions of job responsibilities
Question: How many teachers leave each academic year and what is their reason?	Method - Quantitative data on teachers leaving (existing school data) - Qualitative focus groups Sources - Open-ended surveys on intent to stay/leave/exit interviews

the recommendation and implementation phase. While all team members are not involved in this specific process, team members should have a voice and assigned tasks for all other processes. One way to communicate this is to go back to the Building Collaborative Teams-Action Plan addressed in Chapter 4, where team members come together to assign tasks based on the unique expertise and perspectives they bring to the team.

Implement

When interpreting data, the team will need to discuss and reflect if the measures were appropriate or need to be changed. Suggested questions the team could discuss could be "why have administrators and teachers have severed trust? "or "why is the training not effective?" and "why are the needs of teachers changing?" This provides teams the opportunity to slow down and think about what the organization needs within their individual contexts, which helps in discovering the very specific barrier and supports the identification of appropriate sustainable solutions.

When interpreting the data, teams might consider informal conversations or "check-ins" among team members to build trust and relationships. Connecting research to understand the history is critical as you want to make sure the story you tell is accurate and in fact what you want to work on and so you do not repeat the mistakes as you have in the past. Diverse teams with multiple perspectives are critical to not only understanding the root cause but also helping to identify sustainable solutions within that specific context. Once you gather all the information, you will synthesize the information to gain invaluable insight into how employees are feeling (individual factors), gauge school morale and culture (external factors), and provide ways to measure success. For example, you can use the data analysis visualization table (Table 5.5 and 5.6) to help organize your data. Additionally, you can also use the data reflection tool (Table 5.7) to judge your success in the data collection process.

TABLE 5.5 Data Analysis Visualization

Type of Data	Results 2022–2023	Results 2023–2024	Summary
Quantitative Attrition Data	5.2% of teachers left	5.8% of teachers left	Percentage of teachers leaving is rising by 0.6%
Qualitative Data Focus Exit Interviews	Theme 1: Lack of Resources Theme 2: Little Admin Support Theme 3: Lack of respect	Theme 1: Limited instructional assistance support for SPED. Theme 2: Little Admin Support Theme 3: Lack of Respect	Themes indicate that admin support and a lack of respect for teacher expertise were the biggest factors in teachers leaving the school. This may be due to not understanding different job roles

TABLE 5.6 Data Analysis Visualization Template

Type of Data	Results 2022–2023	Results 2023–2024	Summary

TABLE 5.7 Data Reflection Tool

Focus Topic	Describe the Why	Apply a Quantitative Data System	Apply a Qualitative Data System	Judge Success
Organization Culture/Community	Identifying school needs Giving voice to employees	School Organizational Health Questionnaire (Hart et al., 2000)	Focus groups (5–8 per group)	Did the survey and focus group information come to the same conclusion? Why or why not?
Employee Well-being	Identifies individual and contextual strengths and gaps	Teacher Subjective Well Being Questionnaire (Renshaw et al., 2015)	A subgroup of 10–15 interviews of selected diverse employees	Did the survey and interview data parse out individual and contextual well-being needs? How will you use this information to move forward?

Note: When survey and focus group data results suggest that there are major areas of improvement (i.e., low teacher morale, lack of trust, and high attrition rates), the team must carefully look at each survey domain and parse out themes in focus groups to get a more nuanced understanding of what the root cause is and what to focus on first.

Study

Draw Recommendations and Conclusions

After analyzing your data, you can now draw conclusions and recommendations based on the data analysis interpretations. This will help the team answer key questions to the results of the needs assessment called a root cause analysis. By working to understand the root cause, you are more likely to generate solutions that connect with your needs. The root cause analysis will help you answer core questions from your needs assessment, such as: (a) who the target population is for learning needs and identification of goals moving forward; (b) how relevant is this information to your focus topic; and (c) what groups are best suited to receive training (Table 5.8).

Once data is analyzed, an external collaborator or an identified small leadership group should come up with an implementation plan based on the results. Literature from the fields of implementation science and organizational change (Foundation for Child Development, 2020) suggests that intentional change happens over time and is not immediate. Because change takes time, creating a 1–3-year plan can help embed practices at the individual and systems level, which is critical to increasing results, growth, and positive culture (see more in Chapter 6). The examples used in this chapter (Ishikawa diagram, SWOT) are tools that can be used in an implementation cycle (Bowers et al., 2022). It is critical that team members have a voice in practices that support their growth, and that leaders can voice the policy and research connection to practice and how these connections and practices will be disseminated to policy leaders, districts, leaders, teachers, families, and community members. Understanding how to pick evidence-based practices from needs assessment results can help dismantle power and privilege as we can work together to build more diverse and equitable processes and practices for all involved in educational systems. We will dive deeper into determining solutions and action planning in Chapter 6.

In summary, all organizational structures generate facilitators and barriers of policies, resources, and knowledge – as a team, we can use organized approaches to the complex reality of individual

TABLE 5.8 Root Cause Analysis Format

Root Cause	Strategies I (If…)	Strategies I (Then….)	Strategies II (If…)	Strategies II (Then….)	Outcome	Outcome Measure
Misperceptions of Admin and Teacher Job Roles	Admin and teachers can switch job roles for a day and discuss job roles	Admin and teachers may have a better understanding of decisions being made	Admin meet with teachers one-on-one and in groups to foster trust and build relationships	Teachers will feel respected and heard and be more willing to engage in support	Teachers and admin build trust and understanding of job roles	Percentage of teachers leave decrease Exit interview themes change
Root Cause	Strategies I (If…)	Strategies I (Then….)	Strategies II (If…)	Strategies II (Then….)	Outcome	Outcome Measure

TABLE 5.9 Change Preventers and Facilitators

Change Preventers	Change Facilitators
Change preventers can include: - Focusing solely on challenges or issues - Not picking diverse methods to get a full story - Inviting the whole team to collect and analyze the data together.	Change facilitators can include: - Start with strengths to enhance challenges. - Explore multiple methods and have discussions on what would work best for your context and questions - Use leaders or outside consultants who are trained in assessment and evaluation to support data collection and analysis for ethical standards and confidentiality

contexts that do not include a one-size-fits-all approach. It is important to focus on multidimensional approaches that involve not only individual voices and multiple perspectives but also whole organization strategies that aim to sustain the change you are working so hard to implement (Table 5.9).

Reflection Questions

1. How does your team currently assess needs?
2. How might you use tools such as the SWOT analysis, pulse check, or Ishikawa?
3. What other data sources might provide a holistic understanding of your team's needs?
4. How might your needs assessment inform what you do next?
5. What are data sources your team might consider and how do they align with your current needs?

References

Banerjee, R., & Luckner, J. (2014). Training needs of early childhood professionals who work with children and families who are culturally and linguistically diverse. *Infants & Young Children, 27*(1), 43–59. https://doi.org/10.1097/IYC.0000000000000000

Batz, R., Blanchard, S. B., Rooks-Ellis, D. L., & Stegenga, S. M. (Eds.). (2023). Leadership: Leading from where you are (DEC recommended practices monograph series no. 9). *Division for early childhood.*

Bowers, G., Mertz, P., & Neiles, K. (2022). A systems thinking approach toward meaningful program assessment. ChemRxiv.

Desai, K. J., Desai, M. S., & Ojode, L. (2015). Supply chain risk management framework: A fishbone analysis approach. *SAM Advanced Management Journal, 80*(3), 34. https://link.gale.com/apps/doc/A432064504/AONE?u=anon~27b04b84&sid=googleScholar&xid=582d4c2f

Diener, E., Scollon, C. N., & Lucas, R. E. (2009). The evolving concept of subjective well-being: The multifaceted nature of happiness. In E. Diener (Ed.), *Assessing well-being: The collected works of Ed Diener* (pp. 67–100). Springer Science+Business Media.

Eisner, E. (1994). *The educational imagination: On the design and evaluation of school programs* (3rd ed.). Macmillan.

Foundation for Child Development. (2020). Getting it Right: Using Implementation Research to Improve Outcomes in Early Care and Education. New York, NY: Foundation for Child Development. https://www.fcd-us.org/getting-it-right-using-implementation-research-to-improve-outcomes-in-early-care-andeducation/

Fox, H. B., Walter, H. L., & Ball, K. B. (2023). Methods used to evaluate teacher well-being: A systematic review. *Psychology in the Schools, 60*(10), 4177–4198. https://doi.org/10.1002/pits.22996

Hart, P. M., Wearing, A. J., Conn, M., Carter, N. L., & Dingle, R. K. (2000). Development of the school organisational health questionnaire: A measure for assessing teacher morale and school organisational climate. *The British Journal of Educational Psychology, 70*(2), 211–228. https://doi.org/10.1348/000709900158065

Renshaw, T. L., Long, A. C., & Cook, C. R. (2015). Assessing teachers' positive psychological functioning at work: Development and validation of the Teacher Subjective Wellbeing Questionnaire. *School Psychology Quarterly, 30*(2), 289.

Renshaw, T. L. (2020). Teacher Subjective Wellbeing Questionnaire (TSWQ): Measure and user guide. Open Science Framework. https://osf.io/6548v

Walter, H. L., Spence, C., & Rooks-Ellis, D. (2024). Leading Systems Change: A Framework for Embedding Well-Being EI/ECSE. *Leadership: Leading from where you are* (DEC Recommended Practice Monograph Series No. 9). Division of Early Childhood.

6
Determine Solutions

Chapter 5 presented information on engaging with team members to conduct needs assessment tailored to their context, resources, strengths, and challenges. In this chapter we use our *(a) reflect, (b) plan, (c) implement, and (d) study* process to identify feasible solutions for your individual needs and to identify a root cause, to develop an action plan to achieve solutions that are right for context

Reflect

First, teams can create opportunities to reflect by considering the data that emerged from the specific components of the needs assessment. This is important so that when teams identify solutions, these are solutions that are feasible to implement as they are solutions that are a good match with the needs, strengths, weaknesses, opportunities, and threats of the organization. Let's say you want to go on vacation for your extended family, but you do not know where to go to ensure all vacationers' needs are met. You already have written down everyone's strengths and needs, and how those strengths and needs can be leveraged on the vacation and how they may inhibit activities on the trip. How would you go about finding a destination that works for everyone (kids, adults, grandparents)? Each family member may present various needs related to preferences and mobility.

DOI: 10.4324/9781032673455-6

Just like planning a vacation with a large diverse group of individuals with different needs, leaders must determine solutions based on the needs assessment. Just like you engage a group of diverse individuals to establish needs, strengths, and barriers, you will also gather these individuals or a subgroup of these individuals to reflect upon the data that emerged from the needs assessment. Engaging with different groups to reflect upon the results will be an important step before the team identifies a solution. Reassessing who is at the table and who leaders invite to the table is critical for systems change to occur.

Plan

Once teams have engaged in reflection, they should identify what their goal is. The goal or goals that teams identify can be done using the SMART goal process. SMART stands for **s**pecific, the goal is clearly defined, **m**easurable, make sure you can track progress, **a**ttainable, the ability to reach your goals, **r**elevant, or connected to your abilities, needs, and interests, and **t**ime-bound, should have a specific deadline for reaching your goal. It is important to identify a goal first so that the information that teams explore as they develop their plan aligns with the goal of the team. Once a goal or goals are identified, teams can brainstorm and identify solutions aligned with the data that emerged from the needs assessment. Depending on the area of focus which we discussed in Chapter 5 (what is the most critical need) and the goal, the solution may be related to processes (e.g., retaining teachers, recruiting and maintaining substitute teachers, sharing information), structures (e.g., engaging in effective supervision), or specific practices (e.g., implementing classroom-based practices, curricular decisions, or behavior support). As teams consider solutions particularly related to practice, it is important to note that there are many web-based resources, programs, and professional development providers available. It is imperative that systems commit to consuming those that are aligned with evidence such as evidence-based education (EBE) and evidence-based practices (EBP). EBE and

EBPs are defined as principles of practices that are based on the best available evidence, rather than personal perspectives or opinions (Cruz et al., 2016). For EBEs and EBPs to be identified they must meet high standards of rigor (i.e., See What Works Clearinghouse), have characteristics such as sufficient power, use baseline measures, be randomly assigned, and use clear protocols. Although there is some variability in the definition of an EBE and EBP, the consensus is that the intervention, strategy, program, or curriculum was evaluated with multiple participants by different researchers across various sites, such as differing kindergarten classrooms, with similar effects observed across studies. We look at the collection of studies to help us understand and answer: (a) What works? (b) For whom? (c) Under what conditions? and (d) For which behaviors? EBPs are "justice oriented", and use of EBPs is a social justice action because the "intent is to ensure all children receive high-quality, scientifically proven supports" (Wahman et al., 2023). When we say this practice, strategy, curriculum, or program is evidence-based, does that mean it is effective for all students across behaviors and settings? Not necessarily as not all practices associated with evidence have been researched in every setting. This however does not mean the practice should not be on the table for consideration. This does however require that families, practitioners, educators, and administrators be discerning when reviewing the evidence base. Reflection and decisions based on individual contexts are most important when discussing what is best for students and families. Questions to think about should include, what population is being studied? Is the population of students or adults in our community reflected in this study? If not, why and would this work for your context? If the team decides to move forward, it also means trying the practice and observing how it is working and being willing to change course should that be necessary.

When teams are working toward enhancing a specific system, such as academic or behavioral goals, they will need to find evidence and gather information (Dunst, 2009). Let's say that your nutritionist and trainer advised you to eat a Mediterranean diet, walk for 30 minutes, and get ample sleep, but you realized that you had a fish and nut allergy in the process. You would then have to go back to the nutritionist and ask them to reevaluate your plan to make it more context-specific and attainable to your needs to determine effective solutions. Had your symptoms not been checked, the nutritionist may have suggested something that could have been effective, but also could have been harmful. The same is true when individual practitioners (e.g., teachers) or districts are considering student academic and behavioral outcomes. Evidence should be used to make decisions regarding practices with the best potential to improve outcomes but also be justice-oriented and context-specific. This step may be done by the educator who is working independently to solve a problem in their classroom or by a district that has decided to adopt an evidence-based practice or curriculum to improve academic or behavioral goals.

Identifying Evidence-Based Practices

One way to gather EBPs is to review materials from peer-reviewed sources that have undergone a review process in which experts related to the topic have reviewed, provided extensive feedback, and recommended for publication. Teams might also consider web resources that draw from evidence-based practices. These can be easier for teams to access than peer-reviewed materials as these often require a subscription. Although accessibility is enhanced, web resources should be selected with caution as it is important to ensure the sources being used are based on evidence as opposed to thoughts and opinions. Reputable web resources include Connect Modules, IRIS, and AFFIRM Modules. These are different from web resources such as Teacher Pay Teacher or various blogs. While there may be valuable information on such sites (Teacher Pay Teacher and Blogs), and while some of the information could align with evidence, this is not guaranteed. We have provided some resources and a planning guide that teams may consider as they gather information from specific sources in Table 6.1.

TABLE 6.1 Resource Planning Guide

Evidence-based Practice Resources	Specific Intervention/ Practice	Context and Population Connection (Yes or No?)
What Works Clearinghouse https://ies.ed.gov/ncee/wwc/FWW		
Pennsylvania Evidence Resource Center https://www.evidenceforpa.org/		
Connect Modules https://connectmodules.dec-sped.org/		
IRIS Modules https://iris.peabody.vanderbilt.edu/pd-hours/earn-pd-hours/available-modules/		
AFFIRM Modules https://afirm.fpg.unc.edu/afirm-modules		
Early Childhood Personnel Preparation Center (ECPC) https://ecpcta.org/		

Once teams have identified evidence-based resources aligned with their needs (see Chapter 5), it is important to gather information from these sources. It may be the case that the practice(s) or curricula practitioners are reading about were validated for a setting that does not align with the one in which the practitioner practices (Sandbank et al., 2020). In this case, it is appropriate to either search for materials that are better aligned to the setting in which one practices. If there are not any resources available, the best available resources and practices can be used while recognizing the practice or practices have not yet been validated for one's setting. Again, this does not mean teams should not use this practice, but rather use the existing research that demonstrates promise to inform their practice. Teams might consider Table 6.2 as they gather information related to a specific goal.

TABLE 6.2 Gather Information

Evidence-based Practice Resources	Specific Intervention/ Practice	Context and Population Connection (Yes or No?)
What Works Clearinghouse https://ies.ed.gov/ncee/wwc/FWW	Pre-K Mathematics (Preparing Young Children for School) (September 2023)	Yes, studies support a large Hispanic population, which matches with our current population.

Implement

Moving into the implementation phase, it is important to note that there is no such intervention or practice that is zero-risk. Every practice has unintended consequences or costs and benefits. Regardless of methodology and ethics, teaching children comes with risks. For example, giving a young child who is experiencing a disability 10 hours of intensive interventions per week on top of their other personal and school needs can come with potential risks such as exclusion from peers of the same age but also benefits such as increased development in that skill area. Therefore, when gathering information for implementation, teams need to create an action plan to ensure that not only operational steps are achieved but also ethical obligations to children and families to achieve the desired solution. First, let's look at how a team can decide between practices and interventions to make the best possible decision for your context. Adapted from the National Implementation Research Framework at the University of North Carolina Chapel Hill (2019), your team can use this exploration tool to help decide which program to implement based on your needs. First, you would insert the programs you are comparing, then you would rate the (1) capacity, or the ability to sustain staffing, coaching, training, and evaluations, (2) fit, or alignment with priorities, family and cultural values, organizational structure, and impact on other interventions and initiatives, and (3) need, or perceptions of need from the community, addressing gaps, and disaggregating data indicating population needs. To do this, you will use a 5-point scale with 1 – does

TABLE 6.3 Evidence-Based Practice Comparison Tool

Committee Members
Topic/Subject Area
District/ School:
Date:

	Capacity	Fit	Need
Program 1			
Program 2			
Program 3			

not support/meet capacity, fit, or need, to 5 – strong support for capacity, fit, or need (Table 6.3).

Once a team chooses their EBP for the desired problem of practice, it is crucial that the team moves on to determine a plan to implement the desired practice. This plan is essential to successful implementation, which is the step in systems change that often does not get completed with fidelity, which is why sustainability and quality of practice become extremely challenging.

For each goal you have achieved, you likely had a plan to achieve it. Your goal likely included steps, target dates, and your role (think of planning that family vacation). Successful implementation of solutions traditionally includes these milestones, the dates by when they will be achieved (booking the trip), who will achieve them (spouse/partner), and what types of resources you need to achieve them (money, time, technology). What is needed will depend largely on the selected solution, what the steps are, and the individuals responsible for achieving each step. Resources can support teams to identify a solution, then input the steps to achieve the identified solution, resources needed to achieve the step, individuals responsible, and the target date for completion. Therefore, organizations or teams can use an action plan, which is a document that lays out every task you need to complete to reach that specific goal.

A successful action plan will clearly outline the steps you need to achieve your goal by the designated time frame. You can use an action plan for single or multiple goals. An action plan is critical as it helps all employees and partners see a clear path forward toward goals and anticipated outcomes. An action plan holds individuals accountable and makes it easier to have clear communication and collaboration, stay motivated on a task, and keep your plan schedule within the anticipated timeline and budget. Just like the data collection and analysis process, only a few individuals should be involved in creating the actual plan, but everyone's voice and perspectives should be heard and valued as the group reviews the plan and revises as necessary. Additionally, the level of detail in the plan can vary based on resources, people in charge, and the complexity of the goal itself. Below are the necessary steps needed to complete an action plan.

After teams decide together on the EBP that will be most effective for their context, the team will come together to develop an action plan. An action plan describes the steps your organization will take to meet its objectives through detailed actionable items, processes, individuals carrying out the process and by which date. Developing an action plan helps turn hopes and dreams into reality and increases efficiency and accountability. While developing an action plan may initially seem like more work, it will ultimately increase the likelihood that the identified solution will be achieved. Components of an action plan consist of several components. Some of the components an action plan may include are:

1. Identified solution (what action or changes will occur)
2. Steps to achieve solution (strategies and processes used)
3. Individuals responsible (who will carry out these changes)
4. Resources (what resources are needed to carry out changes? money, staff.)
5. Target dates (by when and for how long?)
6. Communication (who should know what – dissemination of clear information)

The action plan template below can support teams to develop an action plan (Table 6.4). To complete the action plan template, first, teams can identify the solution, steps to achieve the

TABLE 6.4 Action Plan Example

Identified Solution (EBP): Social Emotional Curriculum (K-5)
School Wide EPB: Class-Wide Function-Related Intervention Teams (CW-FIT) (Study Review Protocol) (May 2023) (WWC Tier 1).

Steps to achieve identified solution	Individuals responsible (name people)	Resources needed to achieve step	Target date	Dissemination of Information (What, Where)
Inform personnel on curriculum changes	Leadership	Models of positive, clear, and direct communication strategies	June 2026–September 2026	Email, video, and all staff meeting in September
Order materials for curriculum	Office staff	Intervention website and publisher, budget	June 2026	Email, phone call correspondence
Train leadership and coaching staff	Leadership	Hire trainers	Communication – June 2026 Training – July 2026	Email, school building
Train school staff	Leadership and coaches	Hire trainers or school coaches	Training – August 2026	School building
Continuous coaching	Coaches	Materials, consultants if needed	Ongoing	Continuous clear communication via faculty and families on fidelity

identified solution, individuals responsible, resources needed to achieve the step, and the target date for completion. Next, you will designate resources and responsibilities based on the strengths and needs of the team, and finally, you will monitor the progress or (monitor implementation), which will be discussed further in Chapter 8. See Table 6.4 for an illustration of how an action plan can be created.

Acknowledging education and school-based well-being needs is critical and a large component of lifting staff and educator morale, increasing buy-in, and maintaining positive school culture to increase student learning and behavioral outcomes. Education and school-based well-being should never be a separate component but interwoven within the fabric of the educational system, culture, and practices. Therefore, as teams develop action plans, they can consider how well-being can be incorporated as a step to ensure education and school-based well-being are intertwined. There are many frameworks to help support systems change (i.e., design-based implementation research). When well-being is implemented and embedded at every level (individual, interpersonal, and contextual), it helps to increase continued collaboration among between leaders and staff by creating trust and supports the adoption of evidence-based and culturally responsive practices, as well as increases opportunities for mutually beneficial and respectfully healthy working environments – all that align with the open-systems model approach.

Notice how in the example in Table 6.5 well-being is embedded within the action plan.

Depending on the solution that was identified in the planning phase, the steps, individuals responsible, and resources will differ, but the information needs to be clear and concise, so everyone knows what they are doing and when they are doing it. Table 6.6 provides a template for your team to develop your action plan.

Study

Once the action plan is developed, teams can engage in study by reflecting on the steps and as they engage in the steps within the action plan, determine if the action plan is being delivered in the way that it was intended. In other words, are the steps identified being followed by the individuals responsible and are the resources in place? If so, the action plan is serving its purpose and is effective in supporting teams to implement steps. Other times, teams will notice a plan is not being followed either because the steps are not being implemented or are being implemented by other team members or additional resources are needed. Take the opportunity to determine the effectiveness of the action plan and if any adjustments need to be made, which would take the team back to the reflect phase of the process to determine how teams might overcome challenges associated with not yet implementing the plan as intended.

TABLE 6.5 Example: Action Plan for Embedding Well-being

Focus Topic: Optimize Teacher Well-being and Decrease Attrition
Identified Solution (EBP): Social Emotional Curriculum (K-5)
School Wide EFB: Class-Wide Function–Related Intervention Teams (CW-FIT) (Study Review Protocol) (May 2023) (WWC Tier 1).

Steps to achieve identified solution	Individuals responsible (name people)	Resources needed to achieve step	Target date	Dissemination of information (What, Where)
Inform personnel on curriculum changes	Leadership	Models of positive, clear, and direct communication strategies	June 2026–September 2026	Email, video, and all staff meeting in September
Generate buy-in for professional growth (topics, schedule, groupings)	Surveys and interviews (what do educators need and want) Topics Experts	Professional development specialists Leader	September 2025	Email, surveys
Order materials for curriculum	Office staff	Intervention website and publisher, budget	June 2026	Email, phone call correspondence
Train leadership and coaching staff	Leadership	Hire trainers	Communication – June 2026 Training – July 2026	Email, school building
Train school staff	Leadership and coaches	Hire trainers or school coaches	Training – August 2026	School building
Create Communities of Practice	Establish a problem of practice Identify research and materials needed Group leadership techniques to promote a sense of belonging and increased voice	Professional development specialists Establish a working group that is supported by leaders	October 2025	School and virtual
Continuous coaching for increased curricular fidelity	Coaches	Materials, consultants if needed	Ongoing	Continuous clear communication via faculty and families on fidelity
Ongoing coaching for increased teacher efficacy	Well-being resources Adult learning resources Ways to assess ongoing growth	Well-being coaches Professional Development Coaches	Ongoing, June 2025	Continuous coaching for individual adult learning needs and increased efficacy

TABLE 6.6 Action Plan Template

Identified Solution (EBP):				
Steps to achieve identified solution	*Individuals responsible (name people)*	*Resources needed to achieve step*	*Target date*	*Dissemination of Information (What, Where)*

Conclusion

It is imperative that educational systems (a) brainstorm to and identify solutions with diverse team representation, (b) develop the action plan including both practice-based and education- and school-based well-being needs, and (c) determine the effectiveness of the action plan to prepare for implementation. Table 6.7 includes change preventers and facilitators to support teams as they engage in identifying a solution, action plan, and determine effectiveness.

TABLE 6.7 Change Preventers and Facilitators

Change Preventers	*Change Facilitators*
Change preventers can include:	Change facilitators can include:
- Choosing practices that are not EPBs or allowing educators to use practices without vetting them, - Unintentionally embedding well-being practices within action plans without purpose - Not clearly stating why you are changing practices or interventions or disseminating a plan and checking in with individuals throughout the process of change	- Standardize the approach to picking practices while allowing educators to have a voice in how these practices are differentiated. - Embed well-being at every level of the action plan to support clear, consistent, and compassionate change - Have a pro-active and clear messaging approach for the change in practices to teachers, families, and community members and why it will be beneficial.

Reflection Questions

1. Where are the places that the teams you are a part of gather information?
2. What do the teams you are a part of do upon making decisions about practices you will implement?
3. How might action planning support your team in moving your plans into implementation?
4. How might the resources provided within this chapter support your team?

References

Cruz, J. P., Colet, P. C., Alquwez, N., Alqubeilat, H., Bashtawi, M. A., Ahmed, E. A., & Cruz, C. P. (2016). Evidence-based practice beliefs and implementation among the nursing bridge program students of a Saudi university. *International Journal of Health Sciences, 10*(3), 405–414.

Dunst, C. J., & Trivette, C. M. (2009). Using research evidence to inform and evaluate early childhood intervention practices. *Topics in Early Childhood Special Education, 29*(1), 40-52. https://doi.org/10.1177/0271121408329227

National Implementation Research Network (2019). *The hexagon: An exploration tool.* University of North Carolina at Chapel Hill. https://www.iu13.org/wp-content/uploads/2023/09/NIRN-Hexagon-Discussion-Analysis-Tool-v2.2.pdf

Sandbank, M., Bottema-Beutel, K., Crowley, S., Cassidy, M., Dunham, K., Feldman, J. I., Crank, J., Albarran, S. A., Raj, S., Mahbub, P., & Woynaroski, T. G. (2020). Project AIM: Autism intervention meta-analysis for studies of young children. *Psychological Bulletin, 146*(1), 1–29. https://doi.org/10.1037/bul0000215

Wahman, C. L., Fettig, A., & Zimmerman, K. (2023). Social and emotional intervention research as justice: A case for accountability. *Remedial and Special Education, 44*(5), 423-438. https://doi.org/10.1177/07419325221143761

7

Supporting Implementation of the Solution

In Chapter 6, we discussed identifying a solution and developing an action plan. In this chapter, we will focus on using our *(a) reflect, (b) plan, (c) implement, and (d) study* process to support implementation of the identified solution. Oftentimes, educator practices (e.g., instructional strategies, curricula delivery, program development, collaboration) are a key step or steps of achieving solutions or may be the solution a team has identified (e.g., implement a positive behavior support system within our district). Once teams have identified implementation of a practice as a step to achieve a solution or the solution, specific support resources are necessary, particularly if the solution includes using a practice or practices with fidelity or the way in which the practice or practices were intended to be used. Think about a time you successfully or unsuccessfully accomplished steps to achieve a solution, such as regular gym visits or use of visual schedules in your classroom. If you were successful, it is likely you had a resource in place to achieve your goal, such as people checking in and providing information and feedback (e.g., "You have got this".), technology systems (e.g., monitoring apps), or self-management systems (e.g., checklists) that supported your implementation of each step. Use Table 7.1 to reflect on the professional and/or personal solutions you have identified, accomplished, and what resources might have supported you in attaining these goals.

TABLE 7.1 Brainstorm Solutions Attained and Not Yet Attained

Solutions	Accomplished	Not Yet Accomplished	Resources to Support Attainment

Professional Development

One resource frequently selected by teams, such as school districts, when they have observed a change in student data or when they have identified something like a new curriculum or a new practice to be responsive to student data is professional development. Professional development typically takes the form of a one-size-fits-all district-wide training. A one-size-fits-all district-wide training typically looks like a half-day, one-day, or two-day event in which participants go to a common location or meet via Zoom or Teams to engage in a listening session to receive information and resources related to a specific topic. While professional development can be an effective first step in increasing knowledge, it is highly ineffective in enhancing use of a curriculum or practice for most educators (Hemmeter et al., 2011). There is actually a very small percentage of humans who can take information that was received during a traditional professional development and move that into their practice. Consider the different professional developments you have attended. What were the topics? Which of these practices are you currently using? What resources did you receive beyond the training to use them?

Coaching

One type of resource within the systems change process that has been identified as effective in moving practice to fidelity is coaching. Coaching may occur at the individual and district level.

There are many positive outcomes associated with coaching, and there are various coaching models across fields of study. For example, coaching has been used in the medical community (e.g., Horowitz et al., 2022; Schickedanz et al., 2023) and the education community (e.g., Coogle et al., 2022; Rock et al., 2013; Scheeler et al., 2004). Although there is much we do not know about coaching such as how much coaching is needed to create change or what model is most effective for whom (Boyatzis & Dhar, 2023), we do know there is a common element across effective coaching systems (those that result in some type of observable change and are socially significant), which is the provision of feedback (Coogle et al., 2022; Scheeler et al., 2004). Effective coaching models have included goal setting and action planning, opportunities for the "coach" to observe in the context of the workplace, and opportunities to engage in reflection and receive feedback.

Benefits of coaching include:

- "Client (coachee) satisfaction with their relationship with the coach and the process results from coaching (de Haan et al., 2019).
- The client's intention to act on and expect specific goals results from coaching (Grant et al., 2012; Spence et al., 2008).
- An improved sense of well-being results from coaching (Spence & Grant, 2007).
- A more substantial and coherent personal vision of one's ideal future results from coaching (Mosteo et al., 2016)".

Coaching as an Individual Consumer Versus Organization Consumer

We want to be explicit in stating that we recognize the consumer of this book may be a teacher trying to find a solution for their classroom or a group such as a district or team attempting to improve academic outcomes by adopting an evidence-based curriculum or practice. Identifying coaching as a step to achieve a solution or as the solution can look different depending upon the reader or the context for which one is seeking information. For example, the teacher may be seeking out a reciprocal partner in which they can engage in a coaching relationship, whereas the district may be thinking about how they can train and support a group of leaders to be coaches to move a particular practice to fidelity within their district using a train the trainer type of model. If the train the trainer scenario fits your context, you can use the practices we describe below in this chapter to recruit and train new coaches. Entities (e.g., organizations, schools, districts) will often refer to this group as a "master cadre" of implementers who have demonstrated success with a specific outcome and thus can engage and support new implementers. This is a critical component of implementation science or the transfer of knowledge of a practice to the practice that is being implemented successfully or with fidelity.

The Coaching Cycle

Reflect

As teams consider coaching to support the implementation of a target solution, it will be important to take time to engage in reflection. Teams might reflect on the action plan to ensure they have clarity of the target solution. They might also consider the coaches or coaching processes that are already in place and discuss how those are working. Perhaps there are elements that are working well and others that may need some improvements. Some of the questions below are questions for teams to consider as they reflect upon coaching as a support to implement the solution (Table 7.2).

Plan

Upon engaging in reflection, the next step within our process is plan. During the plan component, teams will identify what is the target solution and how coaching will be implemented to support implementation of the solution.

TABLE 7.2 Reflection Log

Reflection Topics	Documentation Log
What is our identified solution?	
How might coaching support implementation of this solution?	
What coaching processes are already in place and how are they working?	
Who might serve as coaches within our team?	
In what ways might teams find time to support coaches?	

Building Partnerships

Coaching is meant to take place within a supportive partnership in contrast to being evaluative and/or directive. Coaching should include identification of preferences, strengths, and needs of the entity in which coaching is occurring. Preferences may be specific to where individuals or entities (e.g., classrooms, schools, teachers) would like to see the step or solution from the action plan occur, when this might occur (e.g., daily, monthly, hourly), and/or how this might occur (e.g., what types of support are needed to ensure implementation and how frequently are they desired). See Table 7.3 to consider various preferences. It is critical that coaches recognize strengths as they have the unique opportunity to build upon these. Perhaps there are already many excellent and evidence-aligned practices in place or perhaps team members have strong interpersonal skills. These should be recognized and highlighted. Teams should use multiple forms of data to identify needs. Several data collection tools and examples have already been shared, and it is important to highlight once again that teams should continue to recognize the needs of the entity as we want to ensure the coaching partnership is well-aligned. When we recognize the preferences, strengths, and needs of our partners, we can enhance buy-in while building a relationship built upon trust. Recognizing the stressors the team or individual practitioner is experiencing can help when building partnerships to ensure that the coaching relationship is supportive as opposed to directional and evaluative. Using

TABLE 7.3 Preference Check

Preference Assessment	
What is the context in which coaching support will be provided?	- Classroom - One on one with student - Home - Other
What types of resources or support would improve team implementation?	- Information coaching - Professional development - Flyers - Other
How often would you like to receive this support?	- Daily - Weekly - Monthly - Bi-monthly - Other
What other information related to achieving the identified solution should we consider?	

"I hear statements" and asking open-ended questions related to the stressors an educator or district is experiencing can often help clarify the preferences, strengths, and needs. Now would be a good time to refer back to Chapter 4 to gather more ideas regarding relationship building as this can be one of the number one predictors of strong partnerships. Once a partnership is built, there is a cyclical process that occurs to ensure effective coaching. This includes *goal setting, observation, the delivery of feedback, problem-solving, and reflection* (Coogle et al., 2022; Nagro et al., 2022).

Goal Setting

Upon building partnerships, goal-setting should commence. Goal setting is the process in which the specific goal is identified by the coachee with the coach. The coach can have a dialogue with the coachee(s) to collaboratively identify a goal that seems socially significant, feasible, and valuable to the coachee. To support implementation of the action plan discussed in Chapter 6, the goal should be aligned with the goal or a step or steps from the action plan that was previously developed (see Chapter 6). Perhaps coaching is one of the resources needed to achieve one of the steps or one of the steps to achieve the solution or it could even be the actual solution for the district or team that has indicated they would like to adopt a coaching model. Coaches might consider the following questions as they partner with the coachee to identify, clarify, or remind both the coach and coachee of the specific elements related to the solution or steps from the action plan:

- What would you like to see occur?
- When will it occur?
- Who is responsible for what regarding implementation?
- What are the target criteria?
- How often might you like to do this?
- Why do you think this is important?
- Why is this important (function)?

Once the coach and coachee have identified or revisited a goal, they can operationalize it by developing a goal statement. The goal statement should include when they would like to see the goal (when), who will implement what will happen (who), what will happen (what), and why it will happen (function). See the examples in Tables 7.4 and 7.5 for ways in which teams have identified a solution or practice and moved this into identification of how coaches can recall, clarify, or remind the team about the step or solution they are working toward from the action plan by working through a goal identification by answering when, who, and what. This process should align with the action plan and should not take the team in a new direction, but rather be an

TABLE 7.4 Example of an Instructional Support

Identified solution or practice: use of transition supports such as visual cues

When	During periods of transition
Who	Educators
What	Will use visual supports
Function	To create a more organized school environment

Goal (when plus who plus what =): During periods of transition, teachers will use visual supports to create a more organized school environment.

TABLE 7.5 Example of an Instructional Process

Identified solution or practice: new documentation to improve processes when requesting support and documenting support provided	
When	During planning periods
Who	Instructional specialists, principals, teachers, and Board Certified Behavior Analysts (BCBAs)
What	Will use one set of documents to request support and documenting support
Function	To enhance the documentation process
Goal (when plus who plus what =): During planning periods, instructional specialists, principals, teachers, and BCBAs will use one set of documents to request support and document support to enhance the documentation process.	

opportunity to bring team members together, including coaches, to ensure everyone is clear on what it is the team is collaborating on to achieve.

Answering these questions ensures clarity as it relates to the step or solution. Without this information or without revisiting the action plan regularly, it is easy for teams to drift away from supporting the implementation of the step or solution the team identified. Remember coaching is all about supporting the implementation of a solution aligned with preferences, strengths, and needs. Coming back to what the solution and the steps to attain the solution are within the action plan can facilitate quality coaching.

Implement

Upon the reflection and planning phases of our process, teams move into implement. Implement is the transition to engaging in the coaching process.

Observation

Observation allows a coach to gain a better understanding of what is taking place where the team expects to implement the identified step or solution to affirm and suggest new ideas to enhance the quality of the practice or process. Think about a time a friend has sought out your advice within an environment that you are not familiar with or a seasoned educator attempting to provide feedback to a novice teacher regarding a challenging behavior that is occurring in their classroom. There is much information the novice teacher might share like what time of day it is happening and what the behavior looks like and there is much experience the seasoned teacher has, but there is still much that remains unknown regarding the context without observation. By engaging in an observation, the seasoned educator can directly observe what is taking place before and after the challenging behavior, what is happening among peers, and what is happening among educators.

Delivery of Feedback

Upon completing an observation or before the next observation occurs (this depends on the structure the team would like to use), feedback should be prepared and delivered that is aligned again with the step or solution and the goal the team is working toward. The most effective feedback is specific, immediate, affirmative, and suggestive (Scheeler et al., 2004).

Elements of Feedback.

Scheeler et al. (2004) conducted an analysis of multiple studies in which coaching practices were used. They found that the most effective feedback is specific, immediate, affirmative, and suggestive. Feedback should be aligned with a specific step or solution and goal, such as an evidence-based practice that was selected and we learned about in Chapter 6 or a process the team is working toward (e.g., mainstreaming the paperwork process). It should also be delivered as soon as possible. There is no available data suggesting time parameters other than the sooner the better. Feedback should be affirmative or praise the use of selected steps or solutions and goals as we want to recognize and recognize again the transition of ideas into implemented actions, and it should be suggestive to help teams or team members identify other ways to use or enhance the step or solution and goal. There is also research that suggests when we use affirmation statements, it is beneficial to discuss the outcomes associated with use. For example, for a team that is working toward enhancing collaboration across team members during planning time to ensure all voices are heard and a team leader observes the exchange of ideas across team members during a planning meeting, they might comment on how rich the conversation is when there is time to exchange ideas. Intentionally pointing out the actions associated as part of the change process is critical to support and sustain change. See the examples in Table 7.6.

TABLE 7.6 Feedback Examples

Solution the team identified in the action plan: Use of naturalistic learning opportunities such as choice making to provide opportunities for students to practice using expressive language to communicate wants and needs.

Step that was identified from the action plan: Implement peer-to-peer coaching across the school to support teachers in their use of naturalistic language opportunities.

Goal that was identified across team members to recall the action plan: Primary grade teachers will use naturalistic learning opportunities such as choice making to provide opportunities for students to practice using expressive language to enhance response opportunities and student engagement.

Elements of Feedback	*Specific*	*Immediate*	*Suggestive*	*Affirmative*
Definition	Providing feedback that is based on a specific practice or solution	Providing feedback in the moment or upon completing an observation	Providing suggestions on how a specific practice or solution is implemented	Providing praise regarding use of the practice or solution and acknowledging the outcomes associated with use of the practice.
Classroom Examples	"You used the choice making strategy to provide communication opportunities when you provided a choice between the red or blue marker".		"I noticed you have many marker choices for students to complete the project. You might consider providing a choice by asking students if they would like the blue or red marker".	"You used the choice making strategy to provide communication opportunities when you provided a choice between the red or blue marker".

Note: These are examples of each element of effective feedback. Teams and individuals consuming this book should use the type of dialogue that will work best for them.

TABLE 7.7 Feedback Log

Goal:		
Suggestions	Affirmations	Where to gather more information

A feedback log can be used to either deliver feedback or to document what a coach and coachee discussed. See Table 7.7 for an example of what a feedback log might include and look like.

Once a team has committed to coaching and quality feedback, there are choices that can be made. One choice is determining who will be the coaches and coachees. These decisions are team-specific and have much to do with feasibility and sustainability. With some teams, the supervisor is a coach of a group whom they are responsible for supervising and the supervisees are the coachee(s). Other teams might consider peer coaching or self-coaching as they develop a coaching network. Peer coaching entails colleagues providing feedback and coaching to one another, while self-coaching involves reviewing one's own practices through video observation or reflection.

Another decision to make is the mode of delivery. Feedback can be delivered through a variety of modes. As mentioned earlier, we do not yet know which model is most effective for whom under what conditions when it comes to feedback, but we do know feedback is the common element across coaching models and that this feedback has been delivered in a variety of ways using a variety of systems resulting in enhanced use of practice (e.g., Barton et al., 2020; Coogle et al., 2022; Rock et al., 2013; Snyder et al., 2015; Scheeler et al., 2018). The options of feedback delivery provide flexibility when considering which choice might work best or be the most feasible.

There are a variety of models with different modes of delivery represented in the literature. For teams, this decision will be based upon the resources the team has access to as it again relates to feasibility and sustainability. Resources to consider include physical presence, time, money, and access to technologies. For example, observations and feedback can take place face to face where the coach observes the coachee and offers specific feedback upon the observation. Perhaps scheduling and travel time do not allow for the coach to be physically present in real time, but they can be electronically present in real time. If so, the team might consider video conferencing to conduct observations and provide feedback. When real-time observations and feedback is not feasible, videos, text, emails, and digital software or apps can be useful tools to support practice change. For example, the coachee can collect a video sample of practice, send it to the coach, and the coach can provide the coachee with feedback using email, text, or digital apps. The team can also use a combination of approaches where the observation might take place face to face or via video conferencing and feedback is provided in another format. Table 7.8 may be useful for teams as they consider the variety of delivery modes. These can be related to other circumstances such as people, scheduling, resources, and more. This may be a time in which your team revisits Chapter 4 where we discuss teaming for success. The important aspect of problem-solving is that there is time to discuss barriers and time to identify potential solutions to try as coaching is a teamwork activity to support implementation of practices and solutions.

Similar to how you might think about a variety of things when selecting your meal of choice at your favorite restaurant,

TABLE 7.8 Continuum of Choices

Who is providing feedback	How will the observation occur	How is feedback provided	When is feedback provided
Supervisor	Observation	Face to face	After observation
Peer	Video conferencing	Video conferencing	During observation
Self	Video recording	Sent via email	Immediately after observation
		Bluetooth device	

there are also some things for teams to consider when selecting the team's coaching model. In summary, the goal is for the team to implement something that is going to be feasible and sustainable that can be seen as a support and not something that will stress the system.

Study

Upon engaging in the coaching process, teams can begin to study or determine whether the coaching system in place is demonstrating effectiveness.

Problem-Solving

Problem-solving can be a part of the feedback process as it allows the individual delivering and the individual receiving feedback to discuss how the selected practice or solution is working. It may be important to clarify the solution or step and goal and to brainstorm with the coachee to address specific environmental barriers. For example, think about an early intervention practitioner who is partnering with a family to develop an individualized family service plan. The practitioner has expressed experiencing challenges with accessing the format in which the Part C organization has made the individualized family service plan available. In this instance, the individual providing and the individual receiving feedback can discuss potential solutions, which might include accessing the form in a new format or downloading software to make the form more readily accessible.

An example at the high school level might be the teacher who is implementing formative assessment strategies aligned with learning objectives (e.g., white boards, ABCD cards, Think-Pair-Share, and Quick Write). While the teacher is presenting new content, they are concerned about a couple of students who arrive tardy and sleep through class. The teacher and the coach discuss solutions such as providing the students a water break, seating the students closer to the teacher, and checking to make sure the students can get sufficient sleep at home. From both the early intervention and high school examples, we can see that problem-solving can address a variety of barriers that can be in place.

Reflection

Once coaches and coachees have engaged in problem-solving, they can move into reflection. It is important to note that we are in the study component of our process discussing reflection within coaching. Once a specific step or solution has been selected, and as the coaching process is ignited, team members should consider engaging in reflection related to the target solution or step and goal. When reflection is implemented within a coaching process, there is enhanced use of the solutions or steps and goals that have been identified (Nagro et al., 2022). This makes sense as reflection provides teams the opportunity to recall the common understanding of what the solution or step and goal is and what it looks like. Data also suggests reflection is integral to the use of practice as it prompts one to think intentionally about implementation, and thus enhance their use. Although reflection is a critical aspect of implementation, data have also demonstrated that without specific guidance, quality reflection does not occur (Nagro et al., 2022). Therefore, there is a need to consider how teams can support effective reflective practice. Nagro and colleagues have provided a model that suggests enhanced reflective practice (Nagro et al., 2017). The first step within Nagro and colleagues' model (2017) is to consider each action that will occur within the step or solution and goal or identify what each step is and then engage in describe, analyze, apply, and judge as consumers consider implementation for each step of the practice. Describe is providing a definition of the step. Analyze is reasoning why choices were made. Application is identifying how you currently use the step or will use the step, and judge is assessing the success of a decision. See the example in Table 7.9. This example is from the state early intervention team who has a solution to increase family-centered practices across their state. One of the steps they identified to achieve this solution is to implement communities of practice that embed coaching to implement family-centered practice. For each step the state has identified, they have created reflection matrices to provide all practitioners the opportunity to reflect on their practice.

TABLE 7.9 Reflection Matrix

Practices	Describe/provide a description of the practice.	Analyze the use of practice	Judge the success of this practice when you have used it or upon using it in the future.	How have you applied, or will you apply this practice in the future?	Notes
Practitioner recognizes the value of routines	Routines are embedded in everyday life for the families we work with and there are countless times we can use these times for learning and family growth.	I chose to use routines as I now understand how critical they are to supporting the development of young children.	I now have a much better understanding of the importance of implementing this as my priority in every case.	I plan to use this as often as possible because it is so natural for occupational therapy. Activities of daily living are natural routines as they happen daily and are meaningful. By also increasing the engagement of the family and better understanding their unique routines, carryover will happen more organically.	I loved Blake's example in the grocery store. It really showed how just increasing connection and engagement changes everything.
Practitioner identifies child preferences with the family	While the family's preference helps tailor your plan, what is most important is learning the child's preference, because it can be the reason the "perfect" plan won't work.	I chose to identify child preferences as I understand this significantly enhances child engagement.	I think I need to better get to know one of the children I work with because of this key principle. The plans made by myself, and the family haven't been working, so I know something is not jiving well with the child's preference. I now know I need to work harder with the family to figure this out.	By increasing engagement through choice with the child and watching the routines unfold without my assistance, I think we can figure out what is getting in the way of achieving our outcomes.	Since the child cannot verbalize his needs consistently, we will have to use different areas to understand his needs.

(Continued)

TABLE 7.9 (Continued)

Practices	Describe/provide a description of the practice.	Analyze the use of practice	Judge the success of this practice when you have used it or upon using it in the future.	How have you applied, or will you apply this practice in the future?	Notes
Practitioner observes routines	Family performs their routines without thinking about them. By sitting back and watching them unfold, we can learn how best we can help. If we jump in too soon, we will miss something.	I chose to observe routines to get a sense of what the everyday routines were.	I jump in too quickly and need to learn to sit back and watch more. This has been a tough one for me to learn, as we all just want to help as much as we can. But in this case, we will learn more if we watch first.	I plan to explain this to one family I work with, so they understand why I am stepping back. I plan to do this from now on when intervening in a new routine.	I will do this during mealtime and focus on observing the routine as much as possible before stepping in for help. During transitions or at the end, we can go through everything together.
Practitioner specifies strategies aligning with the outcome(s) within routines with the family	As OTs, I think we are constantly thinking about how we can modify and adapt. So, by observing these important routines, we can best see how we can intervene.	I understand that strategies must align with the target I am working toward to support the family and observe progress.	With one family, I saw that they were struggling with the child's fear of the stroller, so we brought the stroller inside and the child helped strap in her stuffed animals and push them around the room. We focused on making it more fun. It went well and they are slowly getting the child used to time in the stroller and getting out in the community by ensuring there are walking breaks out of the stroller as well.	One thing I love to do is figure out how I can modify or adapt a task to make it more accessible. One child I work with struggles with fine motor control and wasn't enjoying using utensils. I found some sensory utensils that hold soft foods (puddings, applesauce) more easily to increase the amount of food help on from the scoop made by the child, so he didn't give up so quickly. He became much more confident in trying to feed himself as a result.	Strategies don't always have to be adaptive equipment, they can be altering a routine timeline, changing the environment, or using preparatory activities such as sensory integration.

TABLE 7.10 Reflective Elements

Goal:				
Identify components of the selected practice	*Describe the component*	*Analyze the choice you made regarding the practice step*	*How do you or will you apply this component*	*How will you judge successful implementation of the practice*

Table 7.10 provides a matrix that you can consider as you implement reflective practice.

To engage in reflection, teams should consider what form of reflection will be most feasible for them to sustain. Think of a time you disliked something or did something that caused a great interruption to your daily life. Chances are you did not continue to do this as it was unpleasant and difficult to implement. Reflection can be done individually, with a partner, with groups of individuals, or through a combination of approaches. Reflection done individually is self-reflection where one is reflecting on their own practice and engaging in this practice independently of others. Peer reflection, however, is a form of reflection where a peer engages in reflection with a partner or small group to share elements of reflection with one another. When video is used in conjunction with reflection, Nagro and colleagues (2022) identify this as video analysis, which provides a tool (video recording) to support reflection.

Reflection can take place right after implementation, although sometimes this is not feasible. In these instances, having tools available to support recollection of implementation may be helpful. For example, delayed reflection may necessitate video recordings of implementation of the solution or practice to use to reflect individually or with a peer or group to determine their description, judgment of application, and their application and future use of the solution or practice.

Tiered Coaching

Researchers recognize that we all need different types and amounts of support to be successful in implementing the solutions or steps and goals we identify (e.g., Coogle et al., 2022). For these reasons, when teams are committed to moving ideas into practice (e.g., implementation of their action plan), they might consider how they can differentiate the coaching support they provide. This often involves a huge mindset shift from "Why is this team member not able to get this" to "What can I do to support this team member be successful". Any time we differentiate or need to change our support to ensure success, we think about intensity. Intensity includes aspects like how frequently or for how long something happens, and it can also include elements such as group size. All people learn new things through providing opportunities to use or practice new skills. If you think about a new skill, you are attempting or have attempted to attain, you might have noticed when you practiced more, you had enhanced outcomes or got better at it. You might have noticed you needed a more tailored learning opportunity where you had more opportunities to practice with feedback like a one-on-one help session in addition to the YouTube tutorial you watched. These are examples of how differentiated supports can help us attain solutions or steps and goals. When a team selects coaching, they might also want to think about what it is that everyone within the team will receive and then what differentiated supports the team have in place to ensure implementation of team members who need increased intensity. Consider how a state system used a tiered approach to support educator's practice in the vignette below.

A state system recognized a need to increase educator's use of family-centered services. They decided that they would not use a one-size-fits-all approach and instead commit to tiered supports. To provide a tiered approach to supporting educators in implementing family-centered services, they developed a tiered model of professional development. Tier one was what all educators would receive. Tier two was what some to the majority or educators would receive, and tier three was what some educators would receive. Which tier of support each educator would receive was based upon the support they needed to move family-centered practices into implementation. Tier one was a webinar that provided an overview of family-centered services. The goal of the webinar was to increase knowledge and included opportunities to engage with other educators through the series of lessons. Because research supports that traditional professional development such as webinars is effective in increasing knowledge, but not practice, leaders knew most educators would need tier two to support transitioning their knowledge to practice. In tier two, educators participated in communities of practice. Each community of practice focused on an element of family-centered practice. Upon completing the lessons within the communities of practice, educators submitted materials that demonstrated their use of the target practices as well as a reflection of the practices. Educators who were using the practices with fidelity (as intended) demonstrated that tier two was the support they needed to transition their knowledge to practice. Those educators who were not yet using the practices received individualized coaching. They were paired with a peer mentor who used the practices described in this chapter to support educators in goal setting, observation, feedback, problem-solving, and reflection. Team leaders found that using a tiered system allowed them to be intentional in their use of resources as educators received the supports they needed to be successful.

Conclusion

In conclusion, accomplishing solutions, steps, and goals often necessitates resources such as coaching to move a practice to fidelity. Quality coaching includes building a partnership, observation, feedback, and reflection. Most importantly, it necessitates a shift in thinking from "Why is this team member not able to get this" to "What can I do to support this team member be successful". Teams have options to consider related to how coaching and reflection might look to increase feasibility and effectiveness and to ensure it is a socially acceptable and significant experience. Table 7.11 provides change preventers and facilitators for teams to consider as they support the implementation of solutions.

TABLE 7.11 Change Preventers and Facilitators

Change Preventers	Change Facilitators
Change preventers can include:	Change facilitators can include:
- Assuming a one size fits all approach - Assuming coaching is impossible because there is no time and no resources available	- Using a tiered approach to provide supports and coaching where they are needed. - Brainstorming about the resources that are available and ways in which teams can leverage the resources and individuals who are a part of the team to support one another

Reflection Questions

1. In what ways does your team currently engage in coaching?
2. Who are the individuals who are a part of your team who can support the implementation of coaching?
3. How might coaching support your team?

References

Barton, E. E., Velez, M., Pokorski, E. A., & Domingo, M. (2020). The effects of email performance-based feedback delivered to teaching teams: A systematic replication. *Journal of Early Intervention*, 42(2), 143–162. https://doi.org/10.1177/1053815119872451

Boyatzis, R. E., & Dhar, U. (2023). When normal is not normal: A theory of the non-linear and discontinuous process of desired change and its managerial implications. *The Journal of Applied Behavioral Science*, 59(3), 364–390. https://doi.org/10.1177/00218863231153218

Coogle, C. G., Nagro, S., Regan, K., O'Brien, K. M., & Ottley, J. R. (2022). The impact of real-time feedback and video analysis on early childhood teachers' practice. *Topics in Early Childhood Special Education*, 41(4), 280–293. https://doi.org/10.1177/0271121419857142

de Haan, E. (2019). A systematic review of qualitative studies in workplace and executive coaching: The emergence of a body of research. *Consulting Psychology Journal: Practice and Research*, 71(4), 227. https://doi.org/10.1037/cpb0000144

Grant, A. M. (2012). Making positive change: A randomized study comparing solution-focused vs. problem-focused coaching questions. *Journal of Systemic Therapies*, *31*(2), 21–35.

Hemmeter, M. L., Snyder, P., Kinder, K., & Artman, K. (2011). Impact of performance feedback delivered via electronic mail on preschool teachers' use of descriptive praise. *Early Childhood Research Quarterly*, *26*(1), 96–109. https://doi.org/10.1016/j.ecresq.2010.05.004

Horowitz, J. M., Choe, M. J., Dienes, K., Cameron, K. A., Agarwal, G., Yaghmai, V., & Carr, J. C. (2022). Team approach to improving radiologist wellness: A case based methodology. *Current Problems in Diagnostic Radiology*, *51*(5), 806–812. https://doi.org/10.1067/j.cpradiol.2022.02.006

Mosteo, L. P., Batista-Foguet, J. M., Mckeever, J. D., & Serlavós, R. (2016). Understanding cognitive-emotional processing through a coaching process: The influence of coaching on vision, goal-directed energy, and resilience. *The Journal of Applied Behavioral Science*, *52*(1), 64–96. https://doi.org/10.1177/0021886315600070

Nagro, S. A., DeBettencourt, L. U., Rosenberg, M. S., Carran, D. T., & Weiss, M. P. (2017). The effects of guided video analysis on teacher candidates' reflective ability and instructional skills. *Teacher Education and Special Education*, *40*(1), 7–25. https://doi.org/10.1177/0888406416680469

Nagro, S. A., Regan, K., Coogle, C., O'Brien, K. M., Raines, A. R., & Wade, C. B. (2022). Promoting reflective ability through a comprehensive field experience that combined video analysis and bug-in-ear coaching. *Journal of Special Education Technology*, *37*(3), 399–412. https://doi.org/10.1177/01626434211022005

Rock, M. L., Schoenfeld, N., Zigmond, N., Gable, R. A., Gregg, M., Ploessl, D. M., & Salter, A. (2013). Can you skype me now? Developing teachers' classroom management practices through virtual coaching. *Beyond Behavior*, *22*(3), 15–23. https://doi.org/10.1177/107429561302200303

Scheeler, M. C., Morano, S., & Lee, D. L. (2018). Effects of immediate feedback using bug-in-ear with paraeducators working with students with autism. *Teacher Education and Special Education*, *41*(1), 24–38. https://doi.org/10.1177/0888406416666645

Scheeler, M. C., Ruhl, K. L., & McAfee, J. K. (2004). Providing performance feedback to teachers: A review. *Teacher Education and Special Education*, *27*(4), 396–407. https://doi.org/10.1177/088840640402700407

Schickedanz, A., Perales, L., Holguin, M., Rhone-Collins, M., Robinson, H., Tehrani, N., Snyder, P. A., Hemmeter, M. L., & Fox, L. (2015). Supporting implementation of evidence-based practices through practice-based coaching. *Topics in Early Childhood Special Education*, *35*(3), 133–143. https://doi.org/10.1177/0271121415594925

Schickedanz, A., Perales, L., Holguin, M., Rhone-Collins, M., Robinson, H., Tehrani, N., ... & Szilagyi, P. G. (2023). Clinic-based financial coaching and missed pediatric preventive care: a randomized trial. *Pediatrics, 151*(3). https://doi.org/10.1542/peds.2021-054970

Spence, G. B., Cavanagh, M. J., & Grant, A. M. (2008). The integration of mindfulness training and health coaching: An exploratory study. *Coaching: An International Journal of Theory, Research and Practice*, *1*(2), 145–163. https://doi.org/10.1080/17521880802328178

Spence, G. B., & Grant, A. M. (2007). Professional and peer life coaching and the enhancement of goal striving and well-being: An exploratory study. *The Journal of Positive Psychology*, *2*(3), 185–194. https://doi.org/10.1080/17439760701228896

Szilagyi, P. G. (2023). Clinic-based financial coaching and missed pediatric preventive care: A randomized trial. *Pediatrics*, *151*(3), e2021054970. https://doi.org/10.1542/peds.2021-054970

8

Evaluate the Process and Solution

Chapter 7 describes how to support implementation of the plan and the solutions generated through the use of reflection on data collected and coaching and feedback. Implementation support is critical to effect change and to ensure sustainability of desired change. As indicated, data play a vital role in supporting implementation and in evaluating the process and the solutions. This chapter describes the *(a) reflect, (b) plan, (c) implement, and (d) study* process as it relates to how to evaluate both implementation and outcomes of the solutions chosen. This is critical to allow the team to adjust or modify the plan or specific actions if something is not working or to recognize successes and celebrate when they occur. Selecting meaningful data to collect that informs decision-making can save time and effort, and result in much more effective implementation of selected solutions and lead to more sustainable change.

Reflect/Plan

To ensure that the team is successful in its efforts to address its goals and vision, it is important to review the initial plan, the action plan we discussed in Chapter 6, and make sure that team members evaluate the process and the solutions. To do this, we return to the root cause analysis and design of the plan where we

DOI: 10.4324/9781032673455-8

identified the cause of the issues faced, our goals, and a plan of action with solutions (see Chapters 5 and 6). Here we also identified the specific solutions and components needed to address the goals along with the desired or expected outcomes. Having a clear understanding and overview of the mechanisms of the change process will help team members to identify what to measure during implementation as well as to evaluate whether change has occurred. Using our process presented earlier (Plan-Implement-Study-Reflect) in the text can help ensure that the evaluation process is focused on measuring the goals of the desired changes and providing the necessary information for making timely adjustments.

Table 8.1 provides a blank copy of Root Cause Analysis that the rural Elementary School described in Chapter 2 used to design their plan, and Table 8.2 includes an example of a completed analysis.

As this example illustrates, the root cause analysis uses data from the needs assessment (in the Elementary School's case: data from a pulse survey and analysis of existing data and behavioral observations using the 5 S framework) to identify both what the team will need to consider in their action plan for implementation and what they will need to measure to evaluate progress. When translating the root cause and suggested solutions into a plan of action as described in Chapter 6, it's important to consider not only who will be responsible for doing each part of the plan but also who will be responsible for monitoring that the essential pieces are completed with fidelity.

TABLE 8.1 Root Cause Analysis Format

Root Cause	Strategies I (If...)	Strategies I (Then...)	Strategies II (If...)	Strategies II (Then...)	Outcome	Outcome Measure

TABLE 8.2 Root Cause Analysis Example

Root Cause	Strategies 1 (If…)	Strategies 1 (Then…)	Strategies 2 (If…)	Strategies 2 (Then…)	Outcome	Outcome Measure
Change in composition of student body	Provide consistent ongoing PD to all staff (teachers, paras and principals) on culturally relevant instruction, universal design for learning (UDL), and positive behavior intervention support (PBIS)	Staff will increase capacity and skills in supporting the needs of students	Teachers implement new skills and strategies in PBIS, Culturally Responsive Instruction (CRI), and UDL with coaching support	Students will display more engaged behavior in class and remain in class for greater periods of time.	Teachers will be able to spend more time teaching. Fewer disruptions to class	Fewer office referrals Fewer referrals for out of school placements Increase in engaged time in class
Lack of staff capacity			Provide ongoing coaching			Increased staff capacity to support diverse students Improved morale

Implement

Fidelity of Implementation Data

Once the solutions have been selected and implemented, it is critical to take data on whether the practices and procedures are being implemented as planned. For example, if the table indicates that teachers are to receive ongoing coaching at least one period a week in which someone comes in their classroom and both models and provides feedback, that should be documented in a coaching log. It is important to use the action plan as a guide regarding who will do what and when. Fidelity is a place to take data on whether the practice was used as planned (e.g., practitioner, activity, practice). For example, if the table indicates that a teacher or paraprofessional will use behavior-specific praise and that takes place during coaching sessions that could be included as a check under a fidelity check in a 5–10-minute observation during this session.

As indicated, setting up and implementing the data collection and monitoring system may be difficult and time-consuming; however, it is critical to the process of change. The team may want to consider what data are already being collected in the school and the extent to which these measure the goals of the plan. If the school is using existing progress monitoring data or benchmark data for baseline data, it may want to continue to use these to monitor progress. More data is not necessarily better. It is easy to overwhelm the team's capacity to both collect meaningful data on implementation of changes and evaluation of changes and, even worse, to reflect regularly and systematically on the meaning of those data. As the team identifies the measures to collect, consideration of which team members will analyze these and when is as important as how and when these will be collected. The team is only able to make data-informed decisions when they have regular and systematic access to the data (Latham et al., 2014; Peddell et al., 2020). The question is how to prioritize which data to collect? This is where it is important to revisit the goals set by the team (see Chapter 6) to identify what performance or actions the team wants to measure. Setting and measuring goals helps clarify expectations, motivate participants, and facilitate celebration of accomplishments.

Many evidence-based curriculum programs include fidelity checklists that can be used by coaches to monitor fidelity. If you are using an evidence-based practice that is not a curriculum, for example, using a form of active responding to increase opportunities to provide formative feedback, or specific individual interventions, then you may want to consider other options to monitor fidelity. In the first situation, with a class-wide intervention, you may want a seating chart, where the coach can check the desks that are perhaps not participating or not receiving the same amount of your attention or are receiving more corrective feedback than affirmative feedback. Depending on the intervention itself, this may provide information as to the type of questions to ask for active responding – perhaps scaffolding with easier, more familiar content to build confidence.

There are also some implementation fidelity checklists that can be individualized for use with function-based behavior plans. Two samples are provided in the Appendix: (a) one for a student who talks out and provides the ways both to act before and after student appropriate and inappropriate behavior; (b) a second is for a student who has difficulty transitioning from one activity to another. Finally, a third blank form is provided that can be individualized for any student. Table 8.3 illustrates another checklist that teams can use, including the steps of a procedure for working with a student, in this case a nonverbal preschool child with autism, teaching him to point. It can obviously be adapted to any skill and used for fidelity monitoring. Table 8.4 includes a blank template for teams.

Implementation/Evaluation Steps Summary

As the team develops its data collection and evaluation plan, team members should consider the following steps:

1. Review the action plan containing the goals
2. Decide on priorities for the evaluation

TABLE 8.3 Implementation Checklist Example

Directions: While observing, place a checkmark next to the items completed.

	Steps	Yes	No
1.	Take student to the back corner of the room and let him move around while working.		
2.	To gain student's attention, play the iPad (PBS Kids). Make sure he cannot easily see the iPad.		
3.	When the student is looking at the iPad, you hit pause.		
4.	After you hit pause, use a short phrase as his direction. For example, "XX, point". The staff member may also use gestural prompting to demonstrate what he should do (you point to the circle while saying "XX, point").		
5.	If the student does the directive, reinforce him by playing the iPad for 5 seconds. If the student does not comply, the staff member should begin at step 2 again.		
6.	Once the student complies, mark the tally to collect data.		
7.	After the student receives his reinforcer (e.g., iPad), repeat the process, beginning at step 2.		
8.	Repeat these steps for 15 minutes.		

TABLE 8.4 Implementation Checklist Format

Directions: While observing, place a checkmark next to the items completed

	Yes	No
1.		
2.		
3.		
4.		
5.		
6.		

3. Develop a data collection plan for process (implementation) and evaluation (outcomes)
4. Determine data collection instruments:
   a. Determine timeline for data collection and analysis along with responsible parties
   b. Collect baseline data as appropriate
   c. Collect fidelity data; provide coaching, retraining or revisit and tweak intervention as needed
   d. Collect pulse/well-being data

Study/Reflect

5. Collect follow-up data:
   a. Analyze and reflect on data; compare to baseline
   b. Analyze and reflect on ongoing pulse data; review with collaborative partners and discuss appropriate strategies to address data.

Reflecting on the data collected is a critical step in the problem-solving framework and is identified in the summary of steps earlier. An important factor to consider when using a problem-solving data-based framework includes ensuring that all collaborative partners are involved in the data sharing and decision-making. The team should use data sharing to discuss and identify possible ways that collaborative structures and processes might improve to facilitate the implementation of the systems change initiative.

Data Collection and Evaluation Plan in Practice

Table 8.3 is a blank format that can be used to translate the goals of the team, root cause analysis, and action plan into a data implementation plan. To consider what this might look like, let's revisit the problem statement from the Elementary School in Chapter 2.

To meet the increasingly diverse needs of students, all teachers, beginning with PK-2 teachers, would participate in ongoing PD and coaching in culturally relevant instruction, engaging and motivating learners and supporting students with diverse needs, and effective classroom management techniques during the school year. The team elected to begin with grades PK-2 where they believed the problems were most challenging and planned to review the data and then scale up to grades 3-5 the following school year.

The vignette provided no specific goals for this, but in this situation, we know that initial issues and concerns arose from high rates of classroom disruptions, high numbers of office referrals, referrals for out-of-school placements, teachers leaving the school, and low teacher morale and capacity to support an increasingly diverse population of students.

School goals would likely include the following:

1. A decrease in classroom disruptions and office referrals for disruptive behavior compared to baseline rates
2. A decrease in referrals for out-of-school behavior compared to baseline (or previous year rates)
3. An increase in student engaged behavior compared to baseline rates
4. An increase in teacher's self-evaluation of capacity, knowledge, and skill in supporting diverse students compared to baseline
5. An increase in teacher morale/well-being and (long-term) teacher retention over time

Table 8.5 illustrates how our elementary school translated their root cause analysis, problem statement, and action plan into a data implementation plan and Table 8.6 provides a template for teams to use. Notice that the implementation of the professional development and coaching for teachers must be completed and monitored for teachers' ability to apply and implement with fidelity before meaningful change in student outcomes should be expected. Data collection initially should focus on baseline data for teachers and students and then on implementation of the process (appropriate implementation of the training and coaching) until teachers are trained.

TABLE 8.5 Data and Implementation Plan Example

Indicator	Who?	What?	When?	Did it occur?
Ongoing training in PBIS, CRI, and UDL	All staff	Kirkpatrick level 1 and 2 evaluations of training (Satisfaction with and Application of)	After each training	
Ongoing coaching	PK-2 teachers	Agreement with statements "Coaching was provided as needed/requested" "I received coaching that was useful in guiding or changing my practice"	Monthly	
Increased capacity and skills in supporting students	All staff	Pulse self-evaluation survey	Quarterly	
Implementation of new skills and support	PK-2 Staff	Coaching observations/fidelity checklist	Quarterly	
Student engagement in class	PK-2 classes	PLACHECK behavioral observation # students engaged – 10 min observations by coaches	Baseline then weekly when coaching implemented	
Office referrals	PK-2 students	# office referrals to principal PK-2 # office referrals other grades	Monthly	
Out of district referrals	All students	# out of district referrals to district office	Semester	
Teacher morale	All Staff	Pulse climate/morale survey	Quarterly	

TABLE 8.6 Data Implementation Plan Format

Indicator	Who?	What?	When?	Did it occur?

TABLE 8.7 Change Preventers and Facilitators

Change Preventers	Change Facilitators
Change preventers can include:	Change facilitators can include:
- Disagreements regarding what data to collect - Collecting too much data that is not meaningful to goals, - Collecting data that is not or cannot be summarized and shared with the team on a regular basis	- Spend time identifying and clearly defining goals as well as how to measure these in a manageable, meaningful way. - Identify who is responsible and when these are to be collected, summarized and shared with the team and faculty and staff to build buy-in. - Take a few minutes at the beginning of staff meetings or assemblies to display graphs of progress toward goals to celebrate and recognize efforts of those collecting and summarizing data

Conclusion

In summary, the data-based process presented here allows collaborative team members to engage in continuous improvement to identify needs, plan and implement solutions, and evaluate change using data to inform and improve both processes and outcomes. As described, the importance of including collaborative partners throughout and carefully identifying goals then using these goals to identify which data to collect may help focus and prioritize both the amount of data to collect and facilitate the feasibility of frequent schedules of and systematic reflection on data analysis and data summaries. Reflections on data should include both comparisons with baseline data and progress toward goals but also discussions about any collaboration issues and barriers and facilitators to progress so that these may also be addressed. Finally, highlight and celebrate improvements; change is hard and even small improvements should be recognized. Table 8.7 includes change preventers and facilitators for teams to consider as they evaluate the process and solution.

Reflection Questions

1. How does your team currently collect data?
2. How might data collection support your team?
3. How might you engage in data collection with your team?

References

Latham, N. (2014). *A practical guide to evaluating systems change in a human services system context*. Center for Evaluation Innovation: Learning for Action. https://www.evaluationinnovation.org/wp-content/uploads/2014/07/Systems-Change-Evaluation-Toolkit_FINAL.pdf

Peddell, L., Lynch, D., Waters, R., Boyd, W., & Willis, R. (2020). How do principals of high-performing schools achieve sustained improvement results? *IAFOR Journal of Education: Studies in Education*, 8(4), 133–149.

9
Sustain Change and Celebrate Success

Thus far, we have been discussing data-based steps to attain systems change. Change takes time and the work to ensure sustainable systems change can be challenging. Systems are complex and team members bring multiple perspectives, areas of expertise, and experiences, which can strengthen systems while also creating obstacles to achieving change when these perspectives, areas of expertise, and experiences differ or conflict with one another. To ensure change is sustainable, it is important that teams celebrate success along the systems change journey and continue to reflect upon the progress they are making together to identify any adjustments that may need to be made to meet team goals.

Think of a milestone you accomplished. Perhaps it was a school project, a half marathon, throwing a successful party, or knitting a blanket. How did you sustain yourself or how did your team sustain themselves to achieve your goal? You likely engaged in incremental steps, followed by periods of "rest", and engaged in the incremental steps again until you reached your goal. Upon reaching your goal, perhaps you felt a sense of accomplishment, or perhaps you celebrated in some way.

Reflect/Plan

As your team engages in systems change, consider how you might gather information to determine the ways in which your team will celebrate success. Remember that success should not be seen as a destination but rather steps along a journey that should be recognized and celebrated. You can also identify how your team will celebrate success and when. You might consider incorporating explicit and intentional conversations about this or your team might more naturally engage in celebrations as they emerge. The most important thing is that teams celebrate in ways that are responsive or meaningful to team members. Have you ever been a part of a team that indicated there would be a party to celebrate your success? Was this something that would be meaningful and valuable to all team members? What about team members who do not really enjoy parties or who do not celebrate in social ways? To be responsive to team members, your team might consider some of these questions to ensure the ways in which the work is recognized is meaningful to each member:

- How does each team member prefer to celebrate accomplishments?
- When have you felt that your contributions and work are valued? What did this look like and when did it occur? Who was present?
- Is there a celebration journey your team might take to engage in smaller and bigger celebrations as you accomplish various team goals?

Teams can address celebration preferences through a conversation, a questionnaire, or survey. Having this information will ensure the celebrations are meaningful to the team members engaged in the work. Consider the following forms you might use in Tables 9.1 and 9.2 or adapt to gather preference information from team members and those impacted by the systems change process.

TABLE 9.1 Sample Rating Form

Name:
Directions: Rate the following celebration preferences in order from 1 as most preferred to X as least preferred. There is also another category for you to identify other celebrations you might prefer.

Celebrations	Rating with 1 being most preferred to X being least preferred
Lunch off campus	
Social outing such as a team dinner or catered lunch	
Class materials stipend	
Class party	
Paid holiday	
Class coverage	
Gratitude wall	
Other	
Other	
Other	

TABLE 9.2 Rating Form Template

Name:
Directions: Rate the following celebration preferences in order from 1 as most preferred to X as least preferred. There is also another category for you to identify other celebrations you might prefer.

Celebrations	Rating with 1 being most preferred to X being least preferred

TABLE 9.3 Celebration Examples

Low Effort/Low-Cost Resources	Example Tasks Completed
Principal offers to teach class for a period during the day Lunch off campus Gratitude wall	Completed developing action plan Identification of an evidence-based practice or curriculum
Medium Effort/Medium Cost Resources	
Principal offers to teach class for a half day Teacher is provided stipend for class materials Peer to peer thank you notes	Completed step in action plan Adopting an evidence-based practice or curriculum
High Effort/High-Cost Resources	
Teacher is provided a paid holiday on day of choice Teaching team lunch Teaching team is provided a stipend for class materials	Completed all steps action plan School-wide implementation of a new curriculum

As you collect preferences, teams might consider Tables 9.3 with examples and 9.4 to use. It is organized into low, medium, and high effort and/or cost resources with examples of how these might be aligned to recognizing accomplishments a team might complete. Teams might consider how they intentionally differentiate celebrations as various team goals are accomplished. The table demonstrates how you might identify low, medium, and high effort and/or cost resources based on various accomplishments. This will likely be different for each team as each team brings diverse resources and context. For this reason, you might consider developing your own low, medium, and high resource-based celebrations specific to your setting and context. Ultimately, the purpose is to keep team

TABLE 9.4 Celebration Template for Teams

Low Effort/Low-Cost Resources	*Example Task Completed*
Medium Effort/Medium Cost Resources	
High Effort/High-Cost Resources	

members motivated, engaged, to ensure they feel the value they bring to the team, and their efforts are recognized. It is also important to consider all who will be impacted by the systems change process and ensure their efforts, work, and outcomes are supported, recognized, and valued in ways that are meaningful to them.

Teams might also consider identifying when these celebrations will occur. For example, your team might schedule monthly meetings in which you will share your data and progress that you are making and use the opportunity to celebrate gains and recognize team members and discuss and brainstorm opportunities to adjust. Sharing data also helps keep everyone on board as they are kept informed of the results of their efforts, the priority, and value placed on their voices being heard. This can dispel the commonly held notion among many teachers in schools about new initiatives that "this too shall pass". The important thing is that teams are responsive to team members and celebrate in regular ways that are meaningful to all who are engaged and recognize the impact within the system.

It can be so easy for teams to focus on the ultimate, long-term goal; however, teams must remember that there are so many steps along the way, and without these steps, the goal cannot take place, so these steps are important to recognize and celebrate. Marathon runners do not show up to the race and run 26.2 miles. They train week after week, each week building upon what they accomplished the previous week. Training can include setbacks such as injury, poor weather conditions, and sickness. These setbacks provide opportunities to pivot to the various circumstances that present themselves. A runner may need to take a week to rest to recover and then adjust their training schedule accordingly to achieve their goal. Similarly, systems change takes time, and we must continuously be prepared to overcome challenges, barriers, and setbacks and recognize accomplishments along the way that lead to the goal to sustain our work! Teams can use materials such as the celebratory planning guide in Table 9.5 to identify the accomplishments, celebrations, target date, and team members involved.

TABLE 9.5 Celebratory Planning Guide

Accomplishments	Celebrations	Target Date	Team Members

Implement/Study

Celebrating success along the way also provides the opportunity to review and reflect on data (Aderet-German & Ben-Peretz, 2020). As you engage in data-based systems change work, as we discussed in Chapter 8, you will be gathering progress monitoring and fidelity data. These forms of data will give you information that your team should consider reflecting upon. As your team reflects upon data, it is important to have intentional conversations about what went well and what could go better as you continue to engage in accomplishing your action plan. This will allow your team to engage in problem-solving together to overcome any hurdles you might face along your systems change journey. It will allow your team to determine how to be more effective as you partner together to achieve common goals. Questions or discussion topics might include:

- What is working well?
- What barriers are you experiencing?
- What successes are you experiencing?
- What support might we as a team consider to enhance our work together?

Your team might consider using resource Table 9.6 to identify successes, barriers, and supports.

TABLE 9.6 Successes, Barriers, and Supports

Goals	Successes related to goal	Barriers to achieving the goal	Supports/resources to overcome barriers

As you engage in these conversations, it is important for all team members to have a safe space in which they can share their unique perspectives. Without preventative measures, some team members may feel uncomfortable and perhaps even become defensive. This is often a result of environments that feel unsafe to some or all team members. This can also be a result of individuals who are experiencing professional insecurities. For these reasons, it is important for teams to continually and intentionally discuss that all teams and systems are a work in progress and there is no perfect team, team member, nor system, thus the need for cyclical systems change process. The most effective teams are those that desire to continue to engage in enhancing systems and can have open, honest, and professional conversations in safe environments. Expressing gratitude for each team member and the unique expertise that they bring can also result in creating a safer environment for all team members.

As you have these conversations, be sure to document how your team will move forward with the information that is shared. What will you do the same? What will you do differently? Remember that systems change is cyclical opposed to linear, and for these reasons, it is critical to take this information, reflect upon it, and explicitly identify what you will do with this information as you move forward (plan, implement, study, and reflect again). Otherwise, these conversations are just conversations that can be identified as "think abouts" and "talk abouts".

There is much great work to do, and we, the authors, are hopeful that your team can use this resource to support your team to accomplish the goals you have identified together. We believe that by (a) identifying a need for change, (b) collaborating

TABLE 9.7 Change Preventers and Facilitators

Change Preventers	Change Facilitators
Change preventers can include:	Change facilitators can include:
- There is not time for celebrations	- Thinking strategically and intentionally to identify celebrations that are meaningful to team members and sustainable

and recognizing the unique strengths of each team member, (c) determining the strengths, weaknesses, opportunities, and threats, (d) identifying a solution and developing an action plan, (e) implementing individualized supports, (f) monitoring progress, and (g) celebrating success along your systems change journey, your team will move thoughts and ideas into practice and overcome an array of challenges that your system may be facing. Table 9.7 identifies change preventers and facilitators for teams to consider as they sustain change and celebrate success.

Reflection Questions

1. How does your team currently celebrate accomplishments?
2. Are these celebrations meaningful to team members or are there ways the team might gather information to determine ways to celebrate that are more meaningful to all team members involved?

References

Aderet-German, T., & Ben-Peretz, M. (2020). Using data on school strengths and weaknesses for school improvement. *Studies in Educational Evaluation, 64*. https://doi.org/10.1016/j.stueduc.2019.100831

Appendix

TABLE 2.3 T-Chart Template

Strengths	Opportunities

TABLE 2.5 5 S Framework Template

S-	Definition	In our school ...
Significance	Purpose for change; why the problem needs to be solved; who is impacted.	
Source	What are the structural, organizational, ideological, capacity, historical, resource, or pedagogical sources of issue?	
Substantive Focus	What should we prioritize? What should we focus on?	
Scale	Who will be involved? Define how many, at what level, and to what extent?	
Scope	Where will this take place? Define the depth and breadth of it within the organization.	

TABLE 4.1 Collaboration Skills – Individual Self Checklist

Activity	Rating 1–3 1–Regularly 2–Sometimes 3–Needs work	How can I improve in this area?
I am respectful even with people that I disagree with.		
I maintain a positive attitude when working as part of a group		
I am fully engaged with the group and contribute willingly		
I accept responsibility (volunteer) for tasks that need to be accomplished		
I enjoy serving in a leadership role		
I am good at active listening and allow others to speak and contribute equally		
I work well with others. Even those different from myself		
I am comfortable giving team members constructive feedback.		
I complete tasks on time		
I stay focused and remain on task		
I make an effort to find time to meet with the team		

TABLE 4.3 Interview Questions – Blank Form

Interview Question	Response
Why are you interested in serving on this team?	
How do you view the role of a team member?	
What skills, expertise, and perspectives could you bring to the team?	
Describe a time when you went above and beyond your duties to help a team reach its goal.	
How should a team member balance transparency and confidentiality?	
How would you describe your communication style?	
How do you handle stress or pressure?	
What motivates you?	
How do you promote diversity, equity, and inclusion in teamwork?	
How would you approach risk assessments in decision-making?	
What do you see as emerging trends in [topic] in education?	

TABLE 4.6 Self-Assessment for Collaborative Teams

Instructions: Using the scale below, rate and describe your current practices and planning time for collaborative teams.

Time for Collaboration

4	3	2	1	Other Comments
We have regular collaborative planning time daily or weekly, built in as part of the school schedule	We have collaborative planning time occasionally (monthly or less) over the course of the school year.	We have collaborative planning time infrequently (PD days) or outside of the school day.	We do not have collaborative planning time.	

Adequate Materials and Resources

4	3	2	1	Other Comments
Our team has access to all necessary materials and resources.	Our team has access to some materials and/or resources and knows how to request additional from the school.	Our team has access to some materials and/or resources but does not have a way to request additional from the school.	Our team does not have access to any necessary materials or resources.	

Clear Articulated Roles and Responsibilities
(e.g., team leader, facilitator, notetaker ...)

4	3	2	1	Other Comments
Our team has a clearly established structure with defined functions, and staff play these roles effectively.	Our team has a clearly established structure with defined functions, but staff does not participate and/or fulfill these roles consistently.	Team members have informal roles and expectations are unclear for how staff should participate or fulfill these roles.	Team members do not have clearly defined roles.	

(Continued)

TABLE 4.6 (Continued)

		Shared Vision and Goals		
4	3	2	1	Other Comments
All participating staff have a shared vision for how collaboration supports improving problems of practice and overall well-being and can articulate a set of clear goals that will help them achieve this vision.	Most participating staff have a shared vision for how collaboration supports improving problems of practice and overall well-being but less can articulate a set of clear goals that will help them achieve this vision.	Less than half of participating staff have a shared vision of how collaboration supports improving problems of practice and overall well-being and there is little consensus around how this vision translates into goals.	There is little to no shared vision of how collaboration supports improving problems of practice and overall well-being.	

TABLE 4.7 Building Collaborative Teams-Action Plan

Directions: Based on your Self-Assessment for Collaborative Teams, identify next steps for how you will support building your team or the adjustments you will make within your current collaborative team structure and a timeline for doing this.

Next Steps	Intended Outcome	Timeline

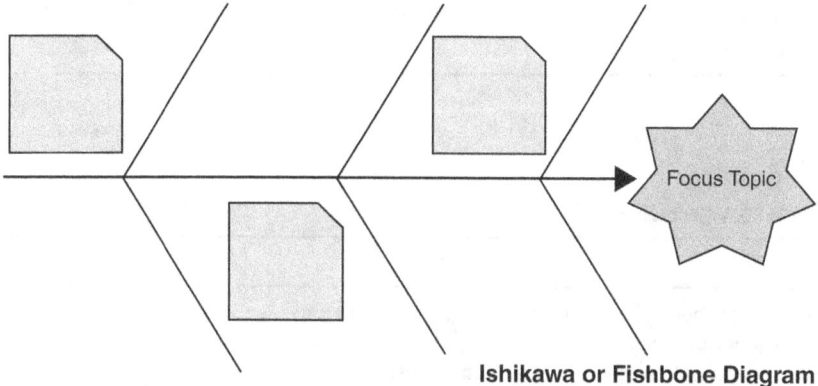

FIGURE 5.2 Fishbone diagram for SWOT analysis: Barriers to success cited in Walter et al., 2024

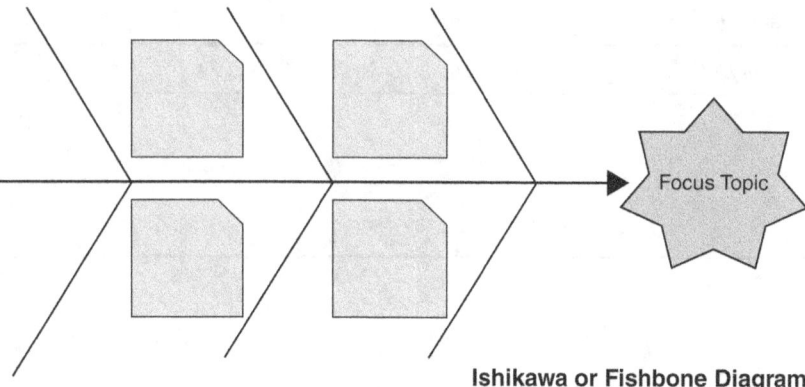

FIGURE 5.3 Fishbone diagram For SWOT analysis: Facilitators to success cited in Walter et al., 2024

TABLE 5.2 SWOT Template

Strengths	Weaknesses
Opportunities	Threats

TABLE 5.3 Checklist for Data Collection Methods

Question	Y/N
Have you been able to access existing data at local and school levels?	
Have you gathered a range of data across a number of academic, social-emotional outcomes, or workplace well-being (i.e., retention of educators)?	
Are there any areas where there is little or no data? Does it exist? How would you obtain this data?	
Do you have a balance of quantitative or qualitative data?	
Have you collected data on target populations?	
Have you collected data across schools or organizations?	
What voices are present and what voices are missing?	

TABLE 5.6 Data Analysis Visualization Template

Type of Data	Results 2022–2023	Results 2023–2024	Summary

TABLE 5.8 Root Cause Analysis Format

Root Cause	Strategies I (If…)	Strategies I (Then…)	Strategies II (If…)	Strategies II (Then…)	Outcome	Outcome Measure
Misperceptions of Admin and Teacher Job Roles	Admin and teachers can switch job roles for a day and discuss job roles	Admin and teachers may have a better understanding of decisions being made	Admin meet with teachers one-on-one and in groups to foster trust and build relationships	Teachers will feel respected and heard and be more willing to engage in support	Teachers and admin build trust and understanding of job roles	Percentage of teachers leave decrease Exit interview themes change
Root Cause	Strategies I (If…)	Strategies I (Then…)	Strategies II (If…)	Strategies II (Then…)	Outcome	Outcome Measure

TABLE 6.1 Resource Planning Guide

Evidence-based Practice Resources	Specific Intervention/ Practice	Context and Population Connection (Y/N?)
What Works Clearinghouse https://ies.ed.gov/ncee/wwc/FWW		
Pennsylvania Evidence Resource Center https://www.evidenceforpa.org/		
Connect Modules https://connectmodules.dec-sped.org/		
IRIS Modules https://iris.peabody.vanderbilt.edu/pd-hours/earn-pd-hours/available-modules/		
AFFIRM Modules https://afirm.fpg.unc.edu/afirm-modules		
Early Childhood Personnel Preparation Center (ECPC) https://ecpcta.org/		

TABLE 6.2 Gather Information

Evidence-based Practice Resources	Specific Intervention/ Practice	Context and Population Connection (Y/N?)
What Works Clearinghouse https://ies.ed.gov/ncee/wwc/FWW	Pre-K Mathematics (Preparing Young Children for School) (September 2023)	Yes, studies support a large Hispanic population, which matches with our current population

TABLE 6.3 Evidence-based Practice Comparison Tool

Committee Members
Topic/Subject Area
District/ School:
Date:

	Capacity	Fit	Need
Program 1			
Program 2			
Program 3			

TABLE 6.6 Action Plan Template

Identified Solution (EBP):				
Steps to achieve identified solution	*Individuals responsible (name people)*	*Resources needed to achieve step*	*Target date*	*Dissemination of Information (What, Where)*

TABLE 7.1 Brainstorm Solutions Attained and Not Yet Attained

Solutions	*Accomplished*	*Not Yet Accomplished*	*Resources to Support Attainment*

TABLE 7.2 Reflection Log

Reflection Topics	*Documentation Log*
What is our identified solution?	
How might coaching support implementation of this solution?	
What coaching processes are already in place and how are they working?	
Who might serve as coaches within our team?	
In what ways might teams find time to support coaches?	

TABLE 7.3 Preference Check

Preference Assessment	
What is the context in which coaching support will be provided?	- Classroom - One on one with student - Home - Other
What types of resources or support would improve team implementation?	- Information Coaching - Professional development - Flyers - Other
How often would you like to receive this support?	- Daily - Weekly - Monthly - Bi-monthly - Other
What other information related to achieving the identified solution should we consider?	-

TABLE 7.7 Feedback Log

Goal:

Suggestions	Affirmations	Where to gather more information?

TABLE 7.10 Reflective Elements

Goal:

Identify components of the selected practice	*Describe the component*	*Analyze the choice you made regarding the practice step*	*How do you or will you apply this component*	*How will you judge successful implementation of the practice*

TABLE 8.1 Root Cause Analysis Format

Root Cause	Strategies I (If…)	Strategies I (Then…)	Strategies II (If…)	Strategies II (Then..)	Outcome	Outcome Measure

TABLE 8.4 Implementation Checklist Format

Directions: While observing, place a checkmark next to the items completed.

	Yes	No
1.		
2.		
3.		
4.		
5.		
6.		

TABLE 8.6 Data Implementation Plan Format

Indicator	Who?	What?	When?	Did it occur?

TABLE 9.2 Rating Form Template

Name:
Directions: Rate the following celebration preferences in order from 1 as most preferred to X as least preferred. There is also another category for you to identify other celebrations you might prefer.

Celebrations	Rating with 1 being most preferred to X being least preferred

TABLE 9.4 Celebration Template for Teams

Low Effort/Low-Cost Resources	Example Task Completed
Medium Effort/Medium Cost Resources	
High Effort/High-Cost Resources	

TABLE 9.5 Celebratory Planning Guide

Accomplishments	*Celebrations*	*Target Date*	*Team Members*

TABLE 9.6 Successes, Barriers, and Supports

Goals	*Successes related to goal*	*Barriers to achieving the goal*	*Supports/resources to overcome barriers*

Additional Resources

Implementation Fidelity Checklist

Student:		Week of:		Setting:	
Observer:	☐ Primary Observer	**TI Start/End Time**	/	**Implementation Fidelity Observation Length**	
	☐ Secondary Observer	**Total Observation time:**			

Key: 0 = *not in place*, 1 = *partially in place*, 2 = *completely in place*

Tactics			Obs 1 _/_/_	Obs 2 _/_/_	Obs 3 _/_/_	Obs 4 _/_/_	Obs 5 _/_/_	Component Total (row)	Component Percent (row)
Antecedent	A1	Reminder seatwork expectations							
	A2	Noncontingent praise provided as AO							
	A3	Prompt to raise hand for help or break							
	A4								
	A5								

(Continued)

Tactics			Obs 1 _/_/_	Obs 2 _/_/_	Obs 3 _/_/_	Obs 4 _/_/_	Obs 5 _/_/_	Component Total (row)	Component Percent (row)
Reinforcement	R1	Attention provided for appropriate request							
	R2	Breakcard given when appropriate							
	R3	Intermittent praise for appropriate bx							
	R4	Stickers/points marked on card							
	R5	Token exchange occurs if Friday							
Extinction	E1	T provides no verbal attention for talkouts							
	E2	T provides no facial negative attention							
	E3	T. provides positive attention to other students for appropriate bx (praise around)							
	E4	Break/Time out not provided for inappropriate bx (student not sent to office)							
	E5								

(Continued)

	Obs 1 _/_/_	Obs 2 _/_/_	Obs 3 _/_/_	Obs 4 _/_/_	Obs 5 _/_/_	Component Total (row)	Component Percent (row)
Tactics							
Teacher initials							
Comments							
Total (Antecedent)							
Percent (Antecedent)							
Total (Reinforcement)							
Percent (Reinforcement)							
Total (Extinction)							
Percent (Extinction)							
Total (A-R-E)							
Percent (A-R-E)							

Fidelity Implementation Checklist

Student:		Week of:		Setting:	
Observer:	☐ Primary Observer	TI Start/End Time	___/___		Fidelity Implementation Observation Length
	☐ Secondary Observer	Total Observation time:			

Key: 0 = *not in place*, 1 = *partially in place*, 2 = *completely in place*

Tactics		Obs 1 _/_/_	Obs 2 _/_/_	Obs 3 _/_/_	Obs 4 _/_/_	Obs 5 _/_/_	Component Total (row)	Component Percent (row)
Antecedent	A1							
	A2							
	A3							
	A4							
	A5							
Reinforcement	R1							
	R2							
	R3							
	R4							
	R5							
Extinction	E1							
	E2							
	E3							
	E4							
	E5							
Teacher initials								
Comments								
Total (Antecedent)								
Percent (Antecedent)								
Total (Reinforcement)								
Percent (Reinforcement)								
Total (Extinction)								

(Continued)

Tactics	Obs 1 _/_/_	Obs 2 _/_/_	Obs 3 _/_/_	Obs 4 _/_/_	Obs 5 _/_/_	Component Total (row)	Component Percent (row)

Percent (Extinction)
Total (A-R-E)
Percent (A-R-E)

Treatment Integrity Checklist

Student:		Week of:		Setting:	
Observer:	☐ Primary Observer	TI Start/End Time	___/___	Treatment Integrity Observation Length	
	☐ Secondary Observer	Total Observation time:			

Key: 0 = *not in place*, 1 = *partially in place*, 2 = *completely in place*

Tactics	Obs 1 _/_/_	Obs 2 _/_/_	Obs 3 _/_/_	Obs 4 _/_/_	Obs 5 _/_/_	Component Total (row)	Component Percent (row)
Antecedent A1							
A2							
A3							
A4							
A5							

(Continued)

Tactics		Obs 1 _/_/_	Obs 2 _/_/_	Obs 3 _/_/_	Obs 4 _/_/_	Obs 5 _/_/_	Component Total (row)	Component Percent (row)
Reinforcement	R1							
	R2							
	R3							
	R4							
	R5							
Extinction	E1							
	E2							
	E3							
	E4							
	E5							
Teacher initials								
Comments								
Total (Antecedent)								
Percent (Antecedent)								
Total (Reinforcement)								
Percent (Reinforcement)								
Total (Extinction)								
Percent (Extinction)								
Total (A-R-E)								
Percent (A-R-E)								

For Product Safety Concerns and Information please contact our EU representative GPSR@taylorandfrancis.com
Taylor & Francis Verlag GmbH, Kaufingerstraße 24, 80331 München, Germany

www.ingramcontent.com/pod-product-compliance
Lightning Source LLC
Chambersburg PA
CBHW070302230426
43664CB00014B/2614